The Big Book of Lap Quilts

The Big Book of
Lap Quilts

51 Patterns for Family Room Favorites

Martingale®
Create with Confidence

The Big Book of Lap Quilts:
51 Patterns for Family Room Favorites
© 2019 by Martingale & Company®

Martingale®
19021 120th Ave. NE, Ste. 102
Bothell, WA 98011-9511 USA
ShopMartingale.com

Printed in China
24 23 22 21 20 19   8 7 6 5 4 3 2 1

Library of Congress Cataloging-in-Publication Data
is available upon request.

ISBN: 978-1-60468-980-8

MISSION STATEMENT

We empower makers who use fabric and yarn
to make life more enjoyable.

CREDITS

PUBLISHER AND
CHIEF VISIONARY OFFICER
Jennifer Erbe Keltner

CONTENT DIRECTOR
Karen Costello Soltys

MANAGING EDITOR
Tina Cook

ACQUISITIONS EDITOR
Karen M. Burns

COPY EDITOR
Jennifer Hornsby

DESIGN MANAGER
Adrienne Smitke

PRODUCTION MANAGER
Regina Girard

COVER AND
INTERIOR DESIGNER
Kathy Kotomaimoce

PHOTOGRAPHER
Brent Kane

ILLUSTRATOR
Sandy Loi

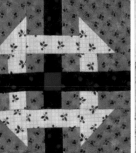

Contents

Introduction

EVERYONE LOVES A LAP QUILT! Endlessly versatile, lap quilts are treasured for so many reasons, from the most practical to the purely aesthetic. They're ideal for cuddling under on the couch, displaying on a wall, draping over a chair—and of course for wrapping around the new baby.

For quilters, the size makes lap quilts especially inviting. They're large enough to give you a real sense of accomplishment and to show off the beautiful fabrics you adore, yet they're small enough to finish in a reasonable amount of time. Lap quilts can be created without breaking the bank or depleting your fabric stash—but they can also help you put a dent in your stash if that's what you'd like to do.

One of the especially nice things about lap quilts is how wonderful they are for gift giving. They're a joy to receive, and so easy for the recipient to display and use. Because they're less labor intensive than a bed quilt, lap quilts are a great way to surprise someone for a birthday or holiday, to celebrate an important milestone, or to provide comfort at a time of need.

This volume is packed with inspiring patterns in a wide variety of styles, so you're sure to find the perfect quilt to give or keep. Enjoy choosing from patchwork, appliqué, and embroidered designs. Express yourself with a planned or scrappy look. Just flipping through the pages to pick your next project is half the fun! Whether you're a beginner or a seasoned quilter, you're in good company with the talented designers whose work appears in this book. They've made sure that these are some of the best quilt designs ever to fall into your lap!

~The Editors at Martingale

Remember Me

CONNIE TESENE AND MARY ETHERINGTON

Album blocks were quite popular in the 1800s. The light centers of the blocks were a place to gather signatures. In this scrappy version, the blocks interlock with splashes of red that form pinwheels. While this project makes a smaller lap quilt, it's perfect for close-up viewing of your family or friends' signatures.

Materials

Yardage is based on 42"-wide fabric.

1⅛ yards total assorted scraps of dark prints for blocks

1⅓ yards of muslin for blocks

⅝ yard total assorted scraps of light prints for blocks

½ yard total assorted scraps of red prints for Pinwheel blocks

⅜ yard of dark blue print for binding

1⅝ yards of fabric for backing

41" × 51" piece of batting

Cutting

All measurements include ¼"-wide seam allowances.

CUTTING FOR 1 ALBUM BLOCK

From *1* of the dark prints, cut:
4 rectangles, 1½" × 3½"
8 squares, 1½" × 1½"

From the muslin, cut:
4 squares, 2½" × 2½"
8 squares, 1½" × 1½"

From *1* of the light prints, cut:
1 rectangle, 1½" × 3½"
2 squares, 1½" × 1½"

CUTTING FOR 1 SEGMENTED ALBUM BLOCK

From *1* of the dark prints, cut:
4 rectangles, 1½" × 3½"
8 squares, 1½" × 1½"

From the muslin, cut:
8 squares, 1½" × 1½"

From *1* of the light prints, cut:
1 rectangle, 1½" × 3½"
2 squares, 1½" × 1½"

CUTTING FOR 1 PINWHEEL BLOCK

From *1* of the red prints, cut:
2 squares, 2⅜" × 2⅜"; cut the squares in half diagonally to yield 4 triangles

From the muslin, cut:
2 squares, 2⅜" × 2⅜"; cut the squares in half diagonally to yield 4 triangles

CUTTING FOR BACKGROUND RECTANGLES

From the muslin, cut:
14 rectangles, 2½" × 3½"

CUTTING FOR BINDING

From the dark blue print, cut:
5 strips, 2½" × 42"

Finished quilt: 37½" × 47½"

Album block: 7" × 7"

Pinwheel block: 3" × 3"

Making the Album Blocks

After sewing each seam, press seam allowances in the directions indicated by the arrows.

Use one light print, one dark print, and muslin for each block.

1 Sew a dark 1½" square between two muslin 1½" squares. Then sew a dark 1½" × 3½" rectangle to the unit. Make four side units.

Make 4.

2 Sew a light 1½" square between two dark 1½" squares. Make two units. Sew a light 1½" × 3½" rectangle between the two units just made. Make one center unit.

Make 1.

3 Join the four side units from step 1, the center unit from step 2, and four muslin 2½" squares. The block should measure 7½" square, including seam allowances. Make 20 blocks.

  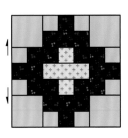

Make 20.

Making the Segmented Album Blocks

1 Repeat steps 1 and 2 for the Album blocks; do not join the units yet.

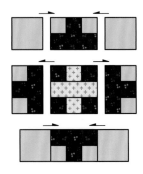

Side units.
Make 4.

Center unit.
Make 1.

2 Join two side units and one center unit. The remaining two side units will be used when arranging the rows. Make 12 blocks that measure 7½" × 3½", including seam allowances.

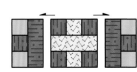 

Make 12.

Making the Pinwheel Blocks

1 Join one red and one muslin 2⅜" triangle. Make four units.

Make 4.

2 Join the four units from step 1. The block should measure 3½" square, including seam allowances. Make 31 blocks.

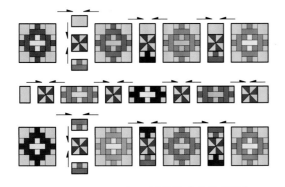

Make 31.

Assembling the Quilt Top

1 Arrange the blocks and muslin 2½" × 3½" rectangles in rows. Make sure to place matching segmented Album blocks together.

2 Sew the units between the Album blocks before joining the row. Sew the blocks and units in rows. Join the rows. Press in one direction.

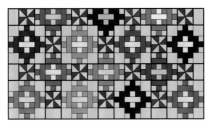

Quilt assembly

Finishing the Quilt

For detailed instructions on any of the finishing steps, go to ShopMartingale.com/HowtoQuilt for free information.

1 Layer the backing, batting, and quilt top; baste.

2 Quilt by hand or machine. The quilt shown is quilted with an allover meander pattern, which is a good choice for a busy and scrappy quilt top.

3 Use the dark blue 2¼"-wide strips to make the binding; attach it to the quilt.

Starry Nights in Winter

CHERYL WALL

Stars are boldly appliquéd in the border and subtly formed at the block intersections in a quilt that's aptly named. The creamy plaid background and the red berries are reminiscent of winterberries contrasting against a snowy backdrop.

Materials

Yardage is based on 42"-wide fabric.

1¼ yards *total* of assorted dark and medium prints and plaids for Nine Patch blocks (collectively referred to as *dark*)

⅞ yard *total* of assorted gold and medium prints for star points and stars (collectively referred to as *gold*)

1½ yards of cream plaid for sashing and border

⅔ yard *total* of assorted light prints for star centers

⅓ yard of dark fabric for vine and leaves

¼ yard of red fabric for berries

½ yard of fabric for binding

3½ yards of backing fabric

62" × 62" piece of batting

1½ yards of 18"-wide fusible web

Black embroidery floss or size 12 pearl cotton

Cutting

All measurements include ¼"-wide seam allowances.

From the assorted dark prints and plaids, cut:

9 sets of 5 matching squares, 3½" × 3½" (45 total)

9 sets of 4 matching squares, 3½" × 3½" (36 total)

12 pairs of matching squares, 3½" × 3½" (24 total)

16 squares, 3½" × 3½"

From the gold prints, cut:

16 sets of 8 matching rectangles, 1½" × 2½" (128 total)

From the cream plaid, cut:

3 strips, 2½" × 42"; crosscut into 24 rectangles, 2½" × 3½"

5 strips, 1½" × 42"; crosscut into 128 squares, 1½" × 1½"

5 strips, 6½" × 42"

From the assorted light prints, cut:

16 sets of matching pieces as follows:
  1 rectangle, 2½" × 4½" (16 total)
  2 rectangles, 1½" × 2½" (32 total)
  12 squares, 1½" × 1½" (192 total)

From the dark fabric, cut:

1¼"-wide bias strips to total 220" in length

From the binding fabric, cut:

6 strips, 2¼" × 42"

Making the Nine Patch Blocks

After sewing each seam, press seam allowances in the directions indicated by the arrows. Choose four matching dark 3½" squares and five matching 3½" squares from a contrasting dark fabric. Arrange the squares in rows as shown. Sew the squares in each row together, and then sew the rows together. Repeat to make nine Nine Patch blocks that measure 9½" square, including seam allowances.

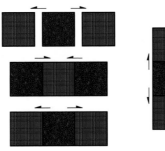 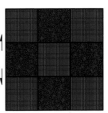

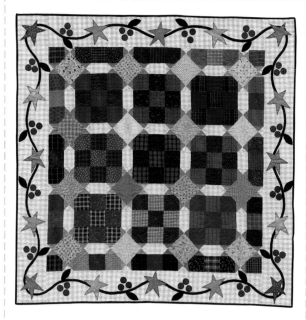

Finished quilt: 53½" × 53½"
Finished block: 9" × 9"

*Pieced and appliquéd by Cheryl Wall;
machine quilted by Mary Flynn*

Piecing the Three-Patch Units

Choose two matching dark 3½" squares and one dark 3½" square of a contrasting fabric. Arrange the squares as shown and sew together. Repeat to make 12 units.

Assembling the Quilt Top

1 Using eight matching gold 1½" × 2½" rectangles, eight cream plaid 1½" squares, and eight light 1½" squares that match the light star center fabric, make four flying-geese units and four reverse flying-geese units as shown. See "Making Flying-Geese Units" on page 15 for more details.

Make 4 of each.

2 Pair a flying-geese unit and a reverse flying-geese unit as shown and sew together. Make four of these units to create the star points—two horizontal star-point units and two vertical star-point units.

3 Sew a light 1½" × 2½" rectangle to each vertical star-point unit as shown.

4 Repeat steps 1–3 to make a set of four star-point units for 16 stars.

5 Using a design wall, a large table, or the floor, lay out the blocks and units. Arrange the Nine Patch blocks, the three-patch units, the star-point units, the light 2½" × 4½" rectangles, the cream plaid 2½" × 3½" rectangles, and the four remaining dark 3½" squares in rows as shown. Rearrange the Nine Patch blocks and the star fabrics/star-point units as desired until you are happy with the placement.

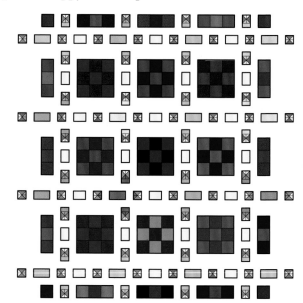

Making Flying-Geese Units

1 Using the squares and rectangles called for in the instructions, place one square over one end of a rectangle, right sides together. Sew diagonally from corner to corner across the square as shown. You can mark the diagonal line on the square if you are more comfortable sewing on a line.

2 Trim away the excess fabric, leaving a ¼" seam allowance. Press the resulting triangle open.

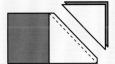
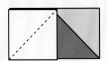

3 Place a second square on the other end of the rectangle, right sides together. Sew diagonally across the square, trim the excess fabric, leaving a ¼" seam allowance, and press.

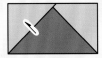

6 Beginning in the upper-left corner, sew four matching light 1½" squares diagonally to one corner each of the 3½" square, two of the three-patch units, and the Nine Patch block as shown. Trim, press the seam allowances toward the Nine Patch block, and return the pieces to the layout.

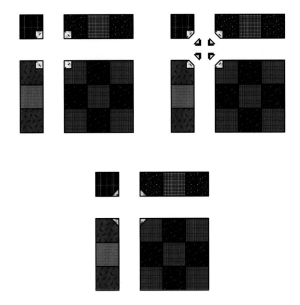

7 Moving to the right, repeat step 6 with the next star fabric, sewing 1½" squares to the corners of two of the three-patch units and two Nine Patch blocks. Continue in this manner, working from left to right across the rows to add squares for all 16 of the stars.

8 Sew the vertical star-point units to the cream plaid 2½" × 3½" rectangles between the Nine Patch blocks, and return them to the layout.

9 Sew the pieces in each row together, and then sew the rows together. The quilt top should measure 41½" square, including seam allowances.

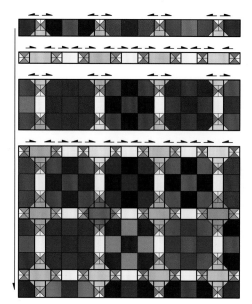

Adding the Border

1 Sew the cream plaid 6½"-wide strips together end to end. Cut two strips, 41½" long, and two strips, 53½" long.

2 Sew the 41½"-long strips to the top and bottom edges of the quilt top. Press the seam allowances toward the border. Sew the 53½"-long strips to the sides of the quilt top and press.

Adding the Appliqués

1 For the vine, sew the dark bias strips together end to end to make one long strip. Fold the strip in half lengthwise, wrong sides together, and sew a scant ¼" seam from the raw edges. Press the seam allowances to the back of the strip.

2 Starting in one corner and using the quilt photo on page 14 for guidance, arrange the bias strip on the border. Pin and appliqué in place. Trim the end of the bias strip, if necessary.

3 Using the red, gold, and dark fabrics and the patterns on page 17, fuse and cut out the appliqué shapes. Make the quantity indicated on the pattern for each shape. Blanket stitch around each shape with two strands of black embroidery floss or one strand of pearl cotton.

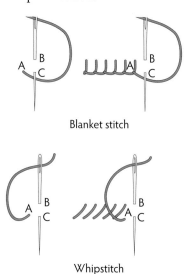

Blanket stitch

Whipstitch

Placing the Appliqués

Use the Nine Patch blocks and stars in the center of the quilt as a grid to aid in placing the bias-strip vine and the appliqué stars and berries.

Finishing the Quilt

For detailed instructions on any of the finishing steps, go to ShopMartingale.com/HowtoQuilt for free information.

1 Layer the backing, batting, and quilt top; baste.

2 Quilt by hand or machine. The quilt shown is quilted with starburst flowers in the Nine Patch blocks and star sashing and has loop-de-loop quilting in the borders.

3 Use the 2¼"-wide strips to make the binding; attach it to the quilt.

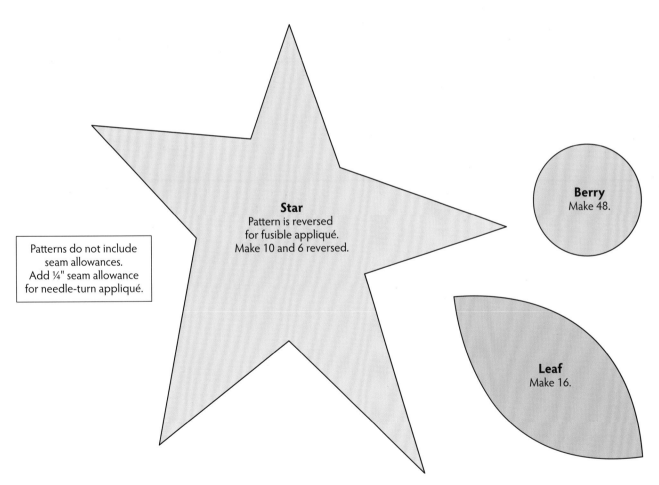

Patterns do not include seam allowances. Add ¼" seam allowance for needle-turn appliqué.

Star
Pattern is reversed
for fusible appliqué.
Make 10 and 6 reversed.

Berry
Make 48.

Leaf
Make 16.

Dripping Diamonds

SARAH BISEL

Create your very own sparkling diamonds using 2½"-wide strips and a simple technique. Whether you use precut strips or strips from your scrap basket, nothing can stop you from having all the diamonds you want.

Materials

Yardage is based on 42"-wide fabric.

39 assorted strips, 2½" × 42"*

¾ yard of blue paisley print for setting triangles

¼ yard of red print for flat piping

2 yards of brown floral for outer border

⅝ yard of fabric for binding

4 yards of fabric for backing

67" × 79" piece of batting

A Jelly Roll has 40 strips, so one roll will work perfectly.

Cutting

All measurements include ¼"-wide seam allowances.

From the blue paisley print, cut:
3 strips, 7½" × 42"

From the red print, cut:
7 strips, 1" × 42"

From the brown floral, cut on the *lengthwise* grain:
4 strips, 6½" × 65"

From the binding fabric, cut:
7 strips, 2½" × 42"

Making the Blocks

After sewing each seam, press seam allowances in the directions indicated by the arrows.

1 Organize your assorted 2½"-wide strips into 13 sets of three strips each. Two strips should be similar in value and the third strip a contrasting value.

2 Piece your strips of three so the middle strip is the contrasting value. Repeat to make 13 strip sets. Press the strips well using a hot iron. Take care not to distort the fabric when pressing. Divide the strip sets into two groups, one group of seven strip sets and one of six.

Prevent Stretching

Use spray starch when pressing the strip sets to help prevent stretching and distortion.

Finished quilt: 61" × 72½"

Finished block: 6" diamond

4 To cut the diamonds, rotate the strip set and line up the 6½" line on your ruler with the 60° angled cut; cut the diamond block and continue to cut each diamond 6½" from the previous cut. Make two cuts, and then check to make sure the 60° angle is still accurate. Trim to fix the angle if necessary, and then continue cutting. You should be able to cut five diamonds from each strip set. Repeat until all strip sets are cut.

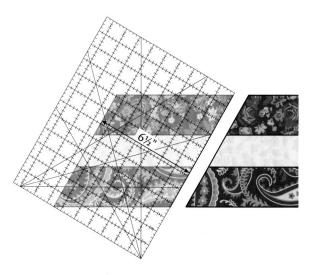

5 For the remaining six strip sets, use the same process as in step 3, but cut a 60° angle in the opposite direction. Cut all six strip sets. You will have several extra diamonds, but this will give you more flexibility and greater variety in your blocks.

3 For the group of seven strip sets, line up the 60° line on the ruler with the top raw edge of the strip set. Accuracy is of the utmost importance. Cut the strip set along the ruler's edge to make a diagonal cut. Repeat until all seven strip sets are cut.

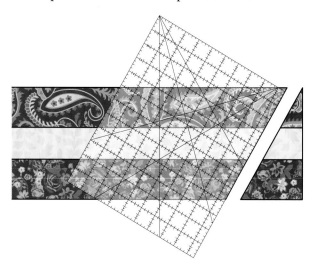

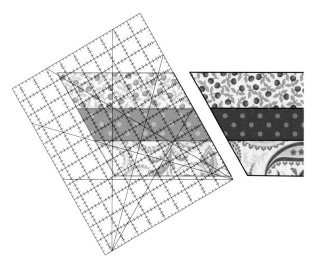

6 From the 7½"-wide blue paisley strips, make a 60° cut (the direction of the angle doesn't matter this time) on one end. Rotate the strip, line up the 7½" line with 60° angled cut, and cut 7½" diamonds. You should be able to cut four per strip, for a total of 12. These setting diamonds are cut larger for ease in piecing.

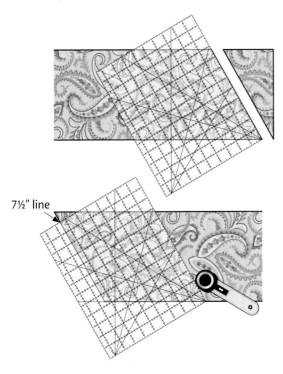

7½" line

7 Cut four of the diamonds from step 6 in half lengthwise (for the sides), and cut eight diamonds in half widthwise (for the top, bottom, and corners).

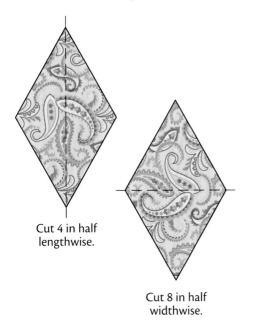

Cut 4 in half lengthwise.

Cut 8 in half widthwise.

Assembling the Quilt Top

1 Arrange the diamond blocks in diagonal rows as shown. Alternate the blocks cut from the seven strip-set group with diamonds cut from the six strip-set group. The rows will have alternating angles that make the blocks look like they are woven.

2 Add the setting pieces, placing the long diamonds on the sides and the equilateral triangles along the top, bottom, and corners.

3 To join the diamond blocks, place them right sides together and line up the raw edges. Align the blocks to make a "valley" ¼" from each edge being pieced. You can insert a pin at the point where the ¼" seam allowances meet to help you line up the blocks.

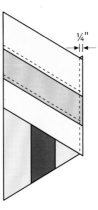

¼"

4 Join the diamonds and setting pieces together into diagonal rows. Repeat until all the rows are assembled. Press.

5 Trim the quilt top ½" beyond each diamond point. Make sure the corners are square.

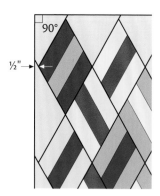

Adding the Flat Piping and Borders

1 For each quilt side, sew two 1"-wide red strips together on the diagonal. Press. Fold the strips in half lengthwise, wrong sides together, and press.

2 Cut one of the 1"-wide strips into two 21"-length strips. For the top piping, sew the 1" × 42" strip to the 1" × 21" strip, on the diagonal. Trim and press. Fold the strip in half lengthwise, wrong sides together, and press. Make two.

3 Using a scant ¼" seam allowance, sew the folded piping to the right side of the top and bottom of the quilt, ensuring that the raw edges are even with the raw edge of quilt. Repeat for the sides. Trim the excess at the corners as needed.

4 Measure the length of the quilt top and trim two of the brown floral strips to this length. Sew the border strips to the left and right sides of the quilt top. Measure the width of the quilt top and trim the remaining brown floral strips to this length. Sew these border strips to the top and bottom of the quilt top and press.

Finishing the Quilt

For detailed instructions on any of the finishing steps, go to ShopMartingale.com/HowtoQuilt for free information.

1 Layer the backing, batting, and quilt top; baste.

2 Quilt by hand or machine. The quilt shown is machine quilted along the diagonal rows in a vine-and-scroll pattern. There is no quilting on the folded piping, and the border is quilted in a vine-and-scroll pattern as well.

3 Use the 2½"-wide strips to make the binding; attach it to the quilt.

Mrs. B

LEONIE BATEMAN

There's just something about four-block appliqué quilts that makes the heart sing. Their design can be so simple, yet they always manage to make a strong statement. This one was made in honor of a wonderful mother-in-law, "Mrs. B."

Finished quilt: 58" × 58"

Designed, machine pieced, hand appliquéd, and hand quilted by Leonie Bateman

Materials

COTTON FABRIC

Yardage is based on 42"-wide fabric.

3⅓ yards of shirting print for appliquéd-block backgrounds and sashing

1⅞ yards of pink print for sashing, cornerstones, and binding

¼ yard of red print for leaf reverse-appliqué inserts

3⅔ yards of fabric for backing

FELTED WOOL FABRIC

Yardage is based on 48"-wide fabric.

1 yard of green for leaves

½ yard of pink for corner flowers and center petals, scalloped center flower, and circle

½ yard of red for corner flowers, scalloped center flower, and center star

12" × 12" piece of antique gold for top of corner flowers

ADDITIONAL MATERIALS

Embroidery floss in colors to match wool fabrics

66" × 66" piece of batting

60" length of freezer paper

Water-soluble glue stick

Stapler

Water-soluble marker (optional)

Cutting

All measurements include ¼"-wide seam allowances.

From the shirting print, cut:

4 squares, 22" × 22"

9 squares, 6½" × 6½"

120 rectangles, 2½" × 6½"

From the pink print, cut:

18 strips, 2½" × 42"; crosscut into 276 squares, 2½" × 2½"

7 strips, 2¼" × 42"

Preparing for Appliqué

1 Fold each shirting-print 22" square in half vertically and horizontally and finger-press the folds. Fold each square in half diagonally in both directions and finger-press the folds. If desired, mark the fold lines with a water-soluble marker.

2 Refer to "Making a Master Pattern" at right to make a master pattern using the patterns on pages 28 and 29.

3 Trace all of the appliqué shapes onto freezer paper, roughly cut out the shapes, and then iron the freezer-paper shapes onto your chosen colors of wool. You'll need four sets of appliqué shapes for the blocks. Refer to the photo on page 23 and the materials list for fabric choices as needed. Cut out the wool shapes.

4 Refer to "Preassembling Units" below to assemble the scalloped center flower into a unit. Refer to "Reverse Appliqué" (page 27) to reverse appliqué the cutout sections of the leaves with the red cotton print.

Preassembling Units

For appliqués that are made up of more than one piece, stitch the pieces together, and then stitch the assembled unit to the background piece. It's easier to stitch one assembled unit to the background than to stitch each piece individually.

Adding the Appliqués

1 Position the appliqués on each of the background squares, working from the bottom layer to the top. Glue and staple your prepared appliqué pieces in place.

2 Using your thread and needle of choice, appliqué the pieces in place with a blanket stitch. Remove the staples.

3 Trim the blocks to 20½" square, keeping the design centered.

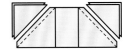

Making a Master Pattern

The appliqué block requires symmetry to achieve a balanced look. The best way to make sure each piece is the same is to make a master pattern. Simply use a pencil to trace the pattern onto a piece of paper (copy paper is fine). You'll then be able to center your background fabric over the master pattern and use it as a guide for placing the appliqués.

Because the pattern is too large to fit on one sheet of paper, you'll need to trace each section onto its own piece of paper, and then join the sections where indicated to make a complete pattern. Be sure to transfer the reference lines to the master pattern.

Making the Sashing

1 Draw a diagonal line from corner to corner on the wrong side of each pink 2½" square.

2 Place marked squares on opposite ends of a shirting-print 2½" × 6½" rectangle as shown. Sew on the marked lines. Trim the seam allowances to ¼". Press the triangles toward the corners. Make a total of 120 sashing units.

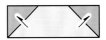

Make 120.

3 Place marked squares on each corner of a shirting-print 6½" square. Sew, trim, and press as before. Make a total of nine cornerstone blocks.

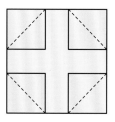 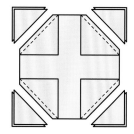

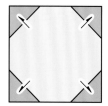

Make 9.

Assembling the Quilt Top

After sewing each seam, press seam allowances in the directions indicated by the arrows.

1 Sew 10 sashing units together as shown to make a sashing strip. Make a total of 12 strips.

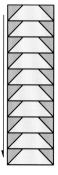

Make 12.

2 Alternately sew three sashing strips and two blocks together as shown. Make a total of two block rows.

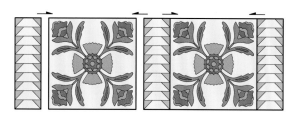

3 Alternately sew three cornerstone blocks and two sashing strips together as shown. Make three strips.

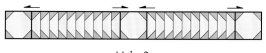

Make 3.

4 Alternately sew the horizontal sashing strips and block rows together to complete the quilt top.

Quilt assembly

Finishing the Quilt

For detailed instructions on any of the finishing steps, go to ShopMartingale.com/HowtoQuilt for free information.

1 Layer the backing, batting, and quilt top; baste.

2 Quilt by hand or machine. The quilt shown is outline quilted around the appliqués, with diagonal lines in the backgrounds of the appliquéd blocks. A Celtic design is quilted in the cornerstone blocks and the sawtooth sashing is outline quilted.

3 Use the pink 2¼"-wide strips to make the binding; attach it to the quilt.

Reverse Appliqué

Reverse appliqué simply means cutting out a section of the main appliqué and slipping another fabric between the background fabric and the appliqué so that a second color shows through. By incorporating these cutout areas, you can easily add extra color and dimension to a design.

1 Make the main shape from wool. Cut away the areas indicated using your embroidery scissors.

2 Cut a piece of wool or cotton that's larger than the main shape and place it under the main shape so that the right side is visible through the cutout areas. Use a couple of dabs of glue and some staples to hold it in place.

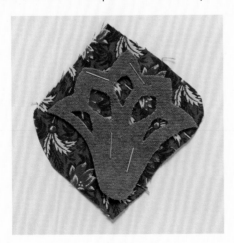

3 Blanket-stitch around the inside edges of the cutout areas to attach the two pieces.

4 Trim the larger background piece so there isn't any fabric showing around the main shape.

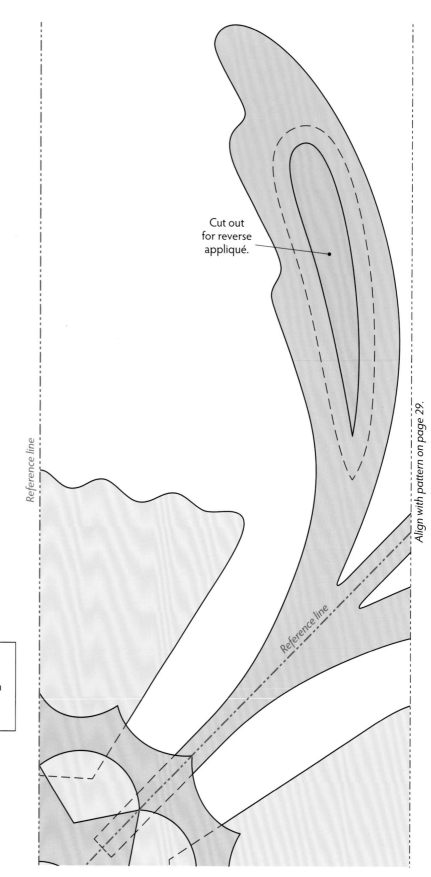

Cut out for reverse appliqué.

Reference line

Reference line

Align with pattern on page 29.

Align patterns as indicated to make a quarter pattern. Make four quarter patterns, and then join pieces to make the complete pattern.

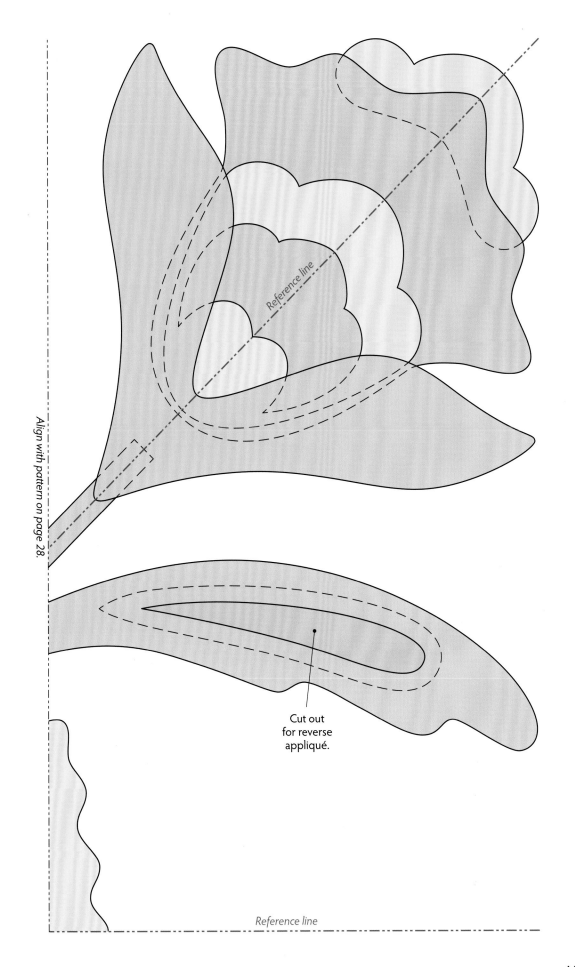

Align with pattern on page 28.

Reference line

Cut out
for reverse
appliqué.

Reference line

Board Game

GERRI ROBINSON

Look closely at this antique-inspired quilt. Not only are the prints reminiscent of yesteryear, but the blocks look like an old-timey Parcheesi board.

Materials

Yardage is based on 42"-wide fabric.

½ yard *total* of assorted red prints for blocks
½ yard *total* of assorted cream and tan prints for blocks (collectively referred to as *tan*)
⅞ yard of cream solid for blocks and sashing
½ yard of red solid for blocks and sashing
1½ yards of red floral for border and binding
3½ yards of backing fabric
59" × 59" piece of batting

Cutting

All measurements include ¼"-wide seam allowances.

From the assorted red prints, cut:
32 squares, 4" × 4"; cut the squares in half diagonally to yield 64 triangles

From the assorted tan prints, cut:
32 squares, 4" × 4"; cut the squares in half diagonally to yield 64 triangles

From the cream solid, cut:
13 strips, 1½" × 42"
64 rectangles, 1½" × 3½"

From the red solid, cut:
8 strips, 1½" × 42"
16 squares, 1½" × 1½"

From the *lengthwise* grain of the red floral, cut:
2 strips, 6½" × 53"
2 strips, 6½" × 41"
4 strips, 2½" × 53"

Making the Blocks

After sewing each seam, press seam allowances in the directions indicated by the arrows.

1 Sew a red triangle to the long side of each tan triangle to make 64 half-square-triangle units. Trim the units to measure 3½" square.

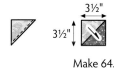

Make 64.

2 Lay out four matching half-square-triangle units, four cream rectangles, and one red square as shown. Sew the pieces together into rows. Join the rows to complete the block. The block should measure 7½" square, including seam allowances. Make a total of 16 blocks.

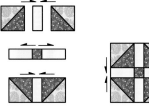

Make 16.

Finished quilt: 49½" × 49½"

Finished block: 14" × 14"

Designed and pieced by Gerri Robinson;
machine quilted by Rebecca Segura

Making the Sashing

1 Sew a cream strip to each long side of a red strip to make a strip set. Make six strip sets. Crosscut the strip sets into 12 sashing strips, 14½" wide. Crosscut the remainder of the strip sets into nine segments, 1½" wide.

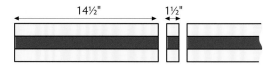

Make 6 strip sets.
Cut 12 segments, 14½" wide,
and 9 segments, 1½" wide.

2 Sew a red strip to each long side of a cream strip to make a strip set. Crosscut the strip set into 18 segments, 1½" wide.

Make 1 strip set.
Cut 18 segments, 1½" wide.

3 Arrange the segments from steps 1 and 2 in Nine Patch blocks as shown. Sew the segments together. The block should measure 3½" square, including seam allowances. Make a total of nine blocks.

Make 9.

3 Sew four blocks from step 2 together to complete the larger block. The block should measure 14½" square. Make four of these blocks.

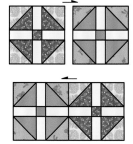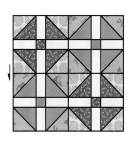

Make 4.

Assembling the Quilt Top

1 Lay out the blocks, the 14½"-wide sashing strips, and the Nine Patch blocks as shown. Sew the pieces together into rows. The quilt center should measure 37½" square, including seam allowances.

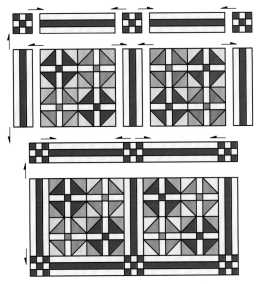

Quilt assembly

2 Measure the length of the quilt top through the center, then trim the two floral 6½" × 41" strips to match that length. Sew the strips to the sides of the quilt top. Measure the width of the quilt top through the center, including the side borders just added, then trim the remaining 6½"-wide strips to that measurement. Sew the strips to the top and bottom.

Finishing the Quilt

For detailed instructions on any of the finishing steps, go to ShopMartingale.com/HowtoQuilt for free information.

1 Layer the backing, batting, and quilt top; baste.

2 Quilt by hand or machine. The quilt shown is quilted with scrollwork and curves in the blocks, serpentine squiggles down the red sashing strips, curves in the Nine Patch blocks, and a feather pattern in the border.

3 Use the red floral 2½"-wide strips to make the binding; attach it to the quilt.

Civil War Log Cabin

CONNIE TESENE AND MARY ETHERINGTON OF COUNTRY THREADS

No quilt block is more American than the humble Log Cabin. In this version, the blocks were arranged with the strong dark-and-light diagonal shading in a straight furrows set, an appropriate tribute for all the farmers and farmhands who fought side by side on our nation's farmlands.

Quilt size: 50" × 66½"
Finished block: 8¼" × 8¼"

Materials

Yardage is based on 42"-wide fabric.

⅛ yard of red fabric for block centers
⅛ yard *each* of 18 light prints for blocks
⅛ yard *each* of 18 medium-light prints for blocks
⅛ yard *each* of 18 medium-dark prints for blocks
⅛ yard *each* of 18 dark prints for blocks
½ yard of black fabric for binding
3⅓ yards of fabric for backing (pieced horizontally)
56" × 72" piece of batting

Cutting

All measurements include ¼"-wide seam allowances. Cutting instructions for Log Cabin blocks are provided on page 36.

From the black fabric, cut:
6 strips, 2¼" × 42"

Making the Log Cabin Blocks

The blocks are made up of rotary-cut pieces, which are indicated by number in the charts on page 36. There are two different blocks: In 24 of the blocks, the last round uses a dark strip and a light strip. In the other 24 blocks, the last round uses a medium-dark strip and a medium-light strip.

For this quilt, blocks were sewn one at a time, and not chain pieced. Note that in each block there are only four different fabrics plus the red center. Of those four different fabrics, each starts as a strip cut 1¼" × 42". The strips are then cut to make each log. Join each log to the block in the order given, pressing the seam allowances toward the log just added.

LOG CABIN BLOCK 1

Cutting instructions are for one block ending with a dark log and a light log. Make 24.

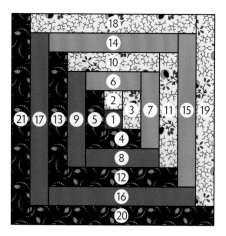

LOG CABIN BLOCK 2

Cutting instructions are for one block ending with a medium-dark log and a medium-light log. Make 24.

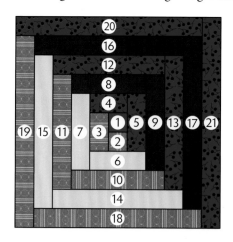

Piece	Fabric	Cutting
1	Red	1¼" × 1¼"
2	Light	1¼" × 1¼"
3	Light	1¼" × 2"
4	Dark	1¼" × 2"
5	Dark	1¼" × 2¾"
6	Medium-light	1¼" × 2¾"
7	Medium-light	1¼" × 3½"
8	Medium-dark	1¼" × 3½"
9	Medium-dark	1¼" × 4¼"
10	Light	1¼" × 4¼"
11	Light	1¼" × 5"
12	Dark	1¼" × 5"
13	Dark	1¼" × 5¾"
14	Medium-light	1¼" × 5¾"
15	Medium-light	1¼" × 6½"
16	Medium-dark	1¼" × 6½"
17	Medium-dark	1¼" × 7¼"
18	Light	1¼" × 7¼"
19	Light	1¼" × 8"
20	Dark	1¼" × 8"
21	Dark	1¼" × 8¾"

Piece	Fabric	Cutting
1	Red	1¼" × 1¼"
2	Medium-light	1¼" × 1¼"
3	Medium-light	1¼" × 2"
4	Medium-dark	1¼" × 2"
5	Medium-dark	1¼" × 2¾"
6	Light	1¼" × 2¾"
7	Light	1¼" × 3½"
8	Dark	1¼" × 3½"
9	Dark	1¼" × 4¼"
10	Medium-light	1¼" × 4¼"
11	Medium-light	1¼" × 5"
12	Medium-dark	1¼" × 5"
13	Medium-dark	1¼" × 5¾"
14	Light	1¼" × 5¾"
15	Light	1¼" × 6½"
16	Dark	1¼" × 6½"
17	Dark	1¼" × 7¼"
18	Medium-light	1¼" × 7¼"
19	Medium-light	1¼" × 8"
20	Medium-dark	1¼" × 8"
21	Medium-dark	1¼" × 8¾"

Assembling the Quilt Top

1 Arrange the blocks in eight rows of six blocks each, alternating blocks 1 and 2, and rotating the blocks to form the diagonal pattern of lights and darks.

2 Sew the blocks together in rows, pressing the seam allowances in opposite directions from row to row. Join the rows. Press the seam allowances in one direction.

Finishing the Quilt

For detailed instructions on any of the finishing steps, go to ShopMartingale.com/HowtoQuilt for free information.

1 Layer the backing, batting, and quilt top; baste.

2 Quilt by hand or machine. The quilt shown is quilted with an allover loop-and-curve pattern.

3 Use the black 2¼"-wide strips to make the binding; attach it to the quilt.

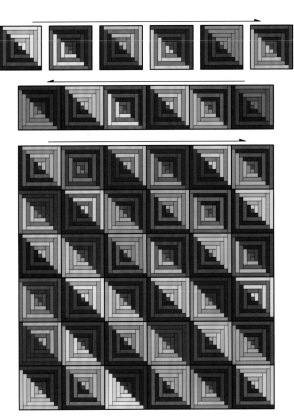

Quilt assembly

Finished quilt: 60½" × 64½"
Finished block: 16" × 20"

Sugar Shack

TONYA ALEXANDER

Make a bold statement with big, bright houses. The quilt top comes together quickly from just 12 blocks with a simple, graphic house design.

Materials

Yardage is based on 42"-wide fabric.

½ yard *each* of assorted tone on tones for houses and backgrounds: pink, aqua, sky blue, light green, dark green, and dark blue

½ yard *each* of 6 assorted light prints for houses and backgrounds

⅔ yard of blue print for binding

4⅛ yards of fabric for backing

69" × 73" piece of batting

Cutting for 1 House Block

All measurements include ¼"-wide seam allowances. The quilt contains 12 House blocks, 6 with light-print backgrounds and tone-on-tone houses, and 6 with tone-on-tone backgrounds and light-print houses. Determine the print pairings before cutting the pieces for each block.

From the house print, cut:
1 rectangle, 4½" × 6½"
3 squares, 3½" × 3½"
2 rectangles, 2½" × 8½"
2 rectangles, 2" × 10½"
1 rectangle, 1½" × 10½"

From the background print, cut:
3 squares, 3½" × 3½"
1 rectangle, 2½" × 16½"
2 rectangles, 2½" × 12½"
2 rectangles, 2½" × 20½"
1 rectangle, 2½" × 6½"
2 squares, 2½" × 2½"
2 rectangles, 1½" × 10½"

From the blue print, cut:
7 strips, 2½" × 42"

Making the House Blocks

After sewing each seam, press seam allowances in the directions indicated by the arrows.

1 Draw a diagonal line from corner to corner on the wrong side of the background 3½" squares. Place a background square right sides together with one house-print 3½" square. Sew ¼" from both sides of the drawn line. Cut along the line to yield two half-square triangles. Trim the units to measure 2½" square. Repeat to make six half-square-triangle units.

Make 6 units.

2 Join the house-print 4½" × 6½" rectangle to the left side of the background 2½" × 6½" rectangle. The unit should measure 6½" square, including seam allowances.

Make 1 unit,
6½" × 6½".

39

5 Lay out the six half-square-triangle units, two background 2½" squares, and two house-print 2½" × 8½" rectangles as shown in two rows. Make sure to orient the half-square-triangle units to create the diagonal lines of the roof. Join the units in each row. The rows should each measure 2½" × 16½", including seam allowances.

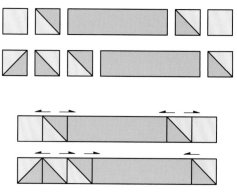

Make 1 of each row,
2½" × 16½".

3 Lay out two house-print 2" × 10½" rectangles and one house-print 1½" × 10½" rectangle alternating with two background 1½" × 10½" rectangles. Join the rectangles along the long edges. The unit should measure 6½" × 10½", including seam allowances.

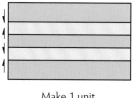

Make 1 unit,
6½" × 10½".

6 Lay out the roof rows, background 2½" × 16½" rectangle, and lower house section in four rows as shown. Join the rows. The house unit should measure 12½" × 16½", including seam allowances.

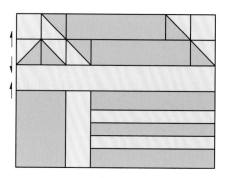

Make 1 unit,
12½" × 16½".

4 Join the unit from step 2 to the left side of the unit from step 3 to make the lower house section, which should measure 6½" × 16½", including seam allowances.

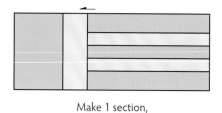

Make 1 section,
6½" × 16½".

7 Sew the background 2½" × 12½" rectangles to the sides of the block. The block should measure 12½" × 20½". Sew the background 2½" × 20½" rectangles to the top and bottom of the block. The block should measure 16½" × 20½", including seam allowances. Repeat to make 12 blocks total.

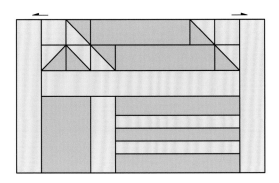

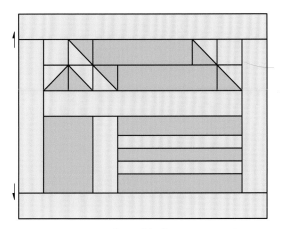

Make 12 blocks, 16½" × 20½".

Assembling the Quilt Top

Lay out the blocks in four rows of three blocks as shown, alternating the light and dark backgrounds. Join the blocks in each row, and then join the rows. The quilt top should measure 60½" × 64½".

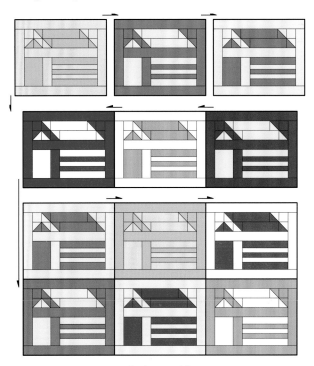

Quilt assembly

Finishing the Quilt

For detailed instructions on any of the finishing steps, go to ShopMartingale.com/HowtoQuilt for free information.

1 Layer the backing, batting, and quilt top; baste.

2 Quilt by hand or machine. The quilt shown is quilted with an allover rectangular stipple pattern.

3 Use the blue 2½"-wide strips to make the binding; attach it to the quilt.

Finished quilt: 65½" × 65½"

Finished block: 9" × 9"

*Pieced by Carrie Nelson;
machine quilted by Diane Tricka*

Cindy Lou Who

CARRIE NELSON

T his is either a Nine Patch quilt with Snowball blocks or a Farmer's Daughter quilt. Maybe it depends on how you place the colors. Either way, it's a pretty neat design, and you can whip up the quilt top in a day or two. Use muted holiday colors for a not-so-obvious Christmas theme.

Materials

Yardage is based on 42"-wide fabric.

48 assorted light, medium, and/or dark 10" squares for blocks*
23 assorted light 10" squares for blocks
½ yard of medium or dark fabric for inner border
⅓ yard *each* of 4 assorted light or medium fabrics for outer border
¾ yard of fabric for binding
4½ yards of fabric for backing
74" × 74" piece of batting

If you want the corners of the 9 Farmer's Daughter blocks to match, you need 9 pairs of 2 matching 10" squares. The remaining 10" squares can all be different.

Cutting

From *each* of the 48 light, medium, and/or dark squares, cut:
2 strips, 3½" × 10"; crosscut each strip into 2 squares, 3½" × 3½" (192 total; 3 are extra)

From *each* of 12 light squares, cut:
1 square, 9½" × 9½" (12 total)

From *each* of 10 light squares, cut:
2 rectangles, 5" × 9½" (20 total)

From the 1 remaining light square, cut:
4 squares, 5" × 5"

From the inner-border fabric, cut:
6 strips, 1½" × 42"

From *each* of the outer-border fabrics, cut:
2 strips, 5" × 42"; crosscut into 4 strips, 5" × 21" (16 total)

From the binding fabric, cut:
280" of 2"-wide bias binding

Assembling the Quilt Top

For the Snowball or Farmer's Daughter blocks, you'll need the following pieces:

- **Triangle corners:** nine sets of eight matching 3½" squares
- **Background:** 12 light 9½" squares and 20 light 5" × 9½" rectangles

For each Nine Patch block, you'll need the following pieces:

- **Corner squares:** four matching 3½" squares (or two sets of two matching squares)
- **Side squares:** four matching 3½" squares
- **Center square:** one coordinating 3½" square

Use a scant ¼"-wide seam allowance throughout. After sewing each seam, press seam allowances in the directions indicated by the arrows, or press them open.

shown. Referring to the photo on page 42 for color-placement guidance, place matching 3½" medium/dark squares in adjacent corners so that there are eight matching squares surrounding nine of the Nine Patch blocks. Each light square will have two matching medium/dark squares in adjacent corners. Pin the medium/dark squares to the light square (or rectangle) so that you can take them to your sewing machine.

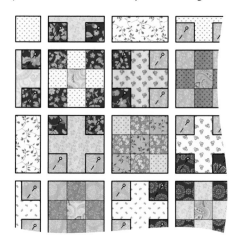

1 To make the Nine Patch blocks, lay out the squares in three rows of three squares each as shown. Sew the squares together in rows, and then sew the rows together. Repeat to make 13 Nine Patch blocks. The blocks should measure 9½" square, including seam allowances.

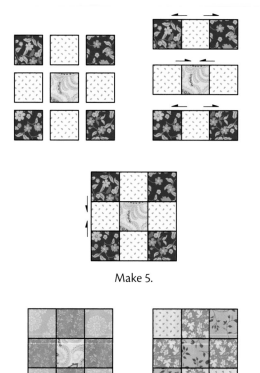

Make 5.

Make 4.   Make 4.

2 On a design wall or large flat surface, lay out the Nine Patch blocks, the 9½" light squares, the 5" × 9½" light rectangles, and the 5" light squares as

3 Draw a diagonal line from corner to corner on the wrong side of the medium/dark squares. Reposition a marked square on the corner of a light square, right sides together and raw edges aligned. Stitch along the drawn line and trim, leaving a ¼" seam allowance. In the same manner, sew marked squares to adjacent corners of the light rectangles. Make the number of units indicated of each color combination.

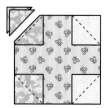

Make 12.

Make 12.

4 Return the pieces to your design wall and carefully examine the layout to make sure each piece is placed correctly. Sew the pieces together into rows. Then sew the rows together and press. The quilt top should measure 54½" square, including seam allowances.

5 Sew the 1½"-wide inner-border strips together end to end. From the long strip, cut two 54½"-long strips and sew them to the sides of the quilt top. Cut two 56½"-long strips and sew them to the top and bottom of the quilt top. (If you trimmed off the pinked edges, cut two strips to 54¼" and two strips to 56¼".) The quilt top should measure 56½" square, including seam allowances.

6 Sew four different 5"-wide outer-border strips together end to end using a diagonal seam. Press

the seam allowances open. Make four border strips. For the side borders, trim two strips to measure 5" × 56½". For the top and bottom borders, trim the remaining two strips to measure 5" × 65½". (If you trimmed off the pinked edges, cut two strips to 56¼" and two strips to 65¼".)

7 Sew the outer-border strips to the sides, and then to the top and bottom of the quilt top.

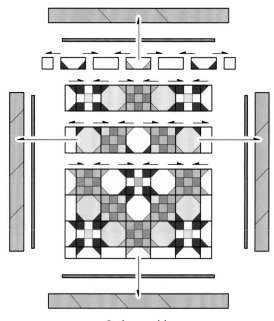

Quilt assembly

Soft and Romantic

Value placement makes all the difference! Give your quilt a different look by placing rose fabrics in an on-point square. Balance the square by using the same rose fabric in the centers of the middle and corner Nine Patch blocks. Arranging all your pieces on a design wall before stitching them together will help you get a look you love.

Pieced by Carrie Nelson; machine quilted by Diane Tricka

Finishing the Quilt

For detailed instructions on any of the finishing steps, go to ShopMartingale.com/HowtoQuilt for free information.

1 Layer the backing, batting, and quilt top; baste.

2 Quilt by hand or machine. The quilt shown is quilted with curved on-point diamonds in the Nine Patch blocks, straight lines in the on-point square, feathers in the light blocks, and triangles and feathers in the borders.

3 Use the 2"-wide strips to make the binding; attach it to the quilt.

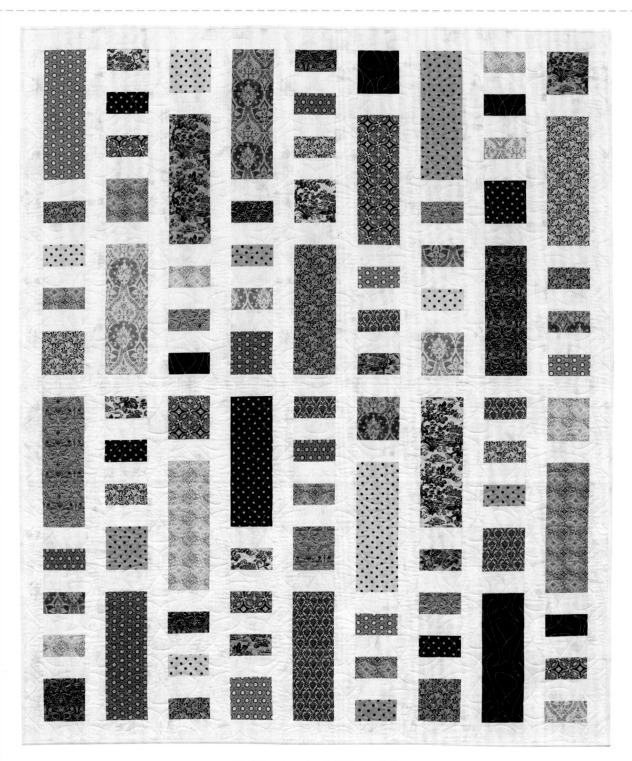

Finished quilt: 56½" × 66½"

Finished blocks: 16" × 30"

Pieced by Susan Guzman;
machine quilted by Linda Barrett

Treble and Bass

SUSAN GUZMAN

This quilt design is a nod to stereos of days gone by. In the days of turntables and eight-track tapes, stereos sometimes had rectangular knobs for controlling the treble and bass. Custom car stereos had panels of small, rectangular lights that would dance to the beat of the music while you cruised along.

The Fabrics

The simple shapes and clean lines of this quilt deliver graphic punch, so look to your fabrics to provide delicate texture. Try mixing dots, florals, and toiles for timeless appeal, or instead emphasize the bold shapes by combining chunky prints or bright solids.

Materials

This pattern is written with directional fabrics in mind so your prints will be upright. Yardage is based on 42"-wide fabric. Fat quarters are 18" × 21".

18 fat quarters of assorted cream, gray, and black prints for blocks
3 yards of mottled cream print for blocks, sashing, borders, and binding
4⅛ yards of fabric for backing
66" × 76" piece of batting

Cutting

All measurements include ¼"-wide seam allowances.

From the *lengthwise* grain of *each* fat quarter, cut:
2 strips, 4½" × 18"; crosscut into:
    1 rectangle, 4½" × 12½" (A; 18 total)
    3 rectangles, 2½" × 4½" (B; 54 total)
    1 square, 4½" × 4½" (C; 18 total)

From the *lengthwise* grain of the mottled cream print, cut:
16 strips, 2½" × 62½"; crosscut *12* of the strips into:
    2 strips, 2½" × 56½"
    39 rectangles, 2½" × 4½" (D)
    12 strips, 2½" × 30½" (E)
    3 strips, 2½" × 16½" (F)

From the *crosswise* grain of the remaining mottled cream print, cut:
5 strips, 2½" × 42"; crosscut into 33 rectangles, 2½" × 4½" (D)
7 strips, 2¼" × 42"

Assembling the Quilt Top

After sewing each seam, press seam allowances in the directions indicated by the arrows. For each block, you'll need three assorted A rectangles, nine assorted B rectangles, and three assorted C squares. You'll also need 12 cream D rectangles and two cream E rectangles.

1 Lay out the A, B, C, and D pieces in three vertical rows as shown. Join the pieces into rows. Sew the rows and E pieces together to complete one block. Make a total of six blocks.

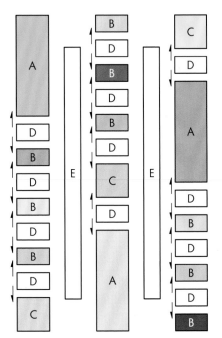

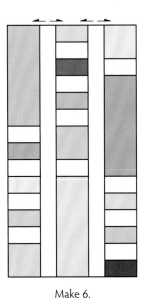

Make 6.

2 Join the blocks and cream F strips as shown, right, to make three vertical rows. Sew the rows and two cream 62½"-long strips together to make the quilt-top center. The quilt-top center should measure 52½" × 62½", including seam allowances.

3 Sew cream 62½"-long strips to opposite sides of the quilt top. Sew cream 56½"-long strips to the top and bottom of the quilt top to complete the border.

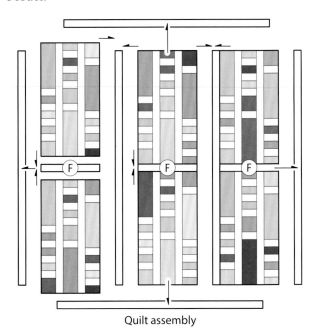

Quilt assembly

Finishing the Quilt

For detailed instructions on any of the finishing steps, go to ShopMartingale.com/HowtoQuilt for free information.

1 Layer the backing, batting, and quilt top; baste.

2 Quilt by hand or machine. The quilt shown is quilted with an allover pattern of loops and swirls.

3 Use the cream 2¼"-wide strips to make the binding; attach it to the quilt.

Four Patch Star

CONNIE TESENE AND MARY ETHERINGTON FOR COUNTRY THREADS

This lap-sized quilt is just the place to display your patriotic colors. Combine red, blue, gray, and cream prints, for a scrappy blend of easy Four Patch blocks and appliquéd stars.

Finished quilt: 43" × 68"

Star block: 12½" × 12½"

Four Patch block: 12½" × 12½"

Materials

Yardage is based on 42"-wide fabric. Fat quarters are 18" × 21".

¼ yard *each* of 8 red prints for star appliqués and Four Patch blocks

8 fat quarters of medium blue prints for circle appliqués

¼ yard *each* of 8 light prints for background of Star blocks and sashing on Four Patch blocks

⅛ yard *each* of 8 dark blue prints for Star blocks and Four Patch blocks

⅜ yard of blue-gray checked fabric for border

⅝ yard of blue plaid for binding

2¾ yards of fabric for backing (pieced horizontally)

49" × 74" piece of batting

Template plastic

Freezer paper or fusible web (optional)

Cutting

All measurements include ¼"-wide seam allowances. Make templates of the star and circle patterns (page 53) and prepare star shapes for hand or fusible appliqué.

From *each* of the red prints, cut:

2 squares, 4¼" × 4¼" (16 total; 2 are extra)

6 squares, 3" × 3" (48 total)

1 star (8 total)

From *each* of the medium blue prints, cut:

1 square, 8" × 8" (8 total)

Continued on page 51

Continued from page 49

From *each* of the light prints, cut:

1 square, 8" × 8" (8 total)

6 squares, 3⅜" × 3⅜"; cut the squares in half
  diagonally to yield 12 triangles (96 total)

4 rectangles, 3" × 8" (32 total; 4 are extra)

3 squares, 3" × 3" (24 total)

From *each* of the dark blue prints, cut:

2 squares, 4¼" × 4¼" (16 total; 2 are extra)

6 squares, 3⅜" × 3⅜"; cut the squares in half
  diagonally to yield 12 triangles (96 total)

3 squares, 3" × 3" (24 total)

From the blue-gray checked fabric, cut:

4 strips, 3" × 42"; crosscut into 16 rectangles, 3" × 8"

From the blue plaid, cut:

2¼"-wide bias strips, enough to yield 224" of binding

Making the Star Blocks

For more information on appliqué techniques, visit ShopMartingale.com/HowtoQuilt for free downloadable instructions. After sewing each seam, press seam allowances in the directions indicated by the arrows.

1 Using your favorite appliqué method, appliqué a star to a medium blue 8" square. When the star is complete, position the circle template over the star, making sure each point of the star is touching the circle edge. Mark and cut out the circle, leaving a narrow turn-under allowance. (Or, if you're using fusible web, cut out the circle on the line after you've applied fusible web to the wrong side of the fabric.) Appliqué the circle/star unit to a light 8" square.

Appliqué star to square.   Mark circle.

2 Using 12 light triangles that match the star background from step 1 and a set of 12 matching dark blue triangles, sew the triangles together to make 12 half-square-triangle units. Sew the half-square-triangle units together in rows of three as shown. Make four rows.

Make 12 matching.

Make 4 rows.

3 Sew rows of triangles to opposite sides of the appliqué block, with the light triangles adjoining the block.

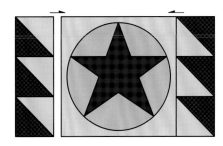

4 On the remaining two triangle rows, sew a red 3" square to the light end of the row and a light 3" square to the blue end of the row. Sew these strips to the top and bottom of the unit from step 3. The block should measure 13" square, including seam allowances. Make eight blocks.

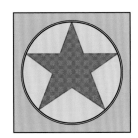
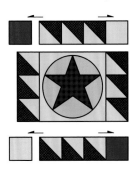

Make 8.

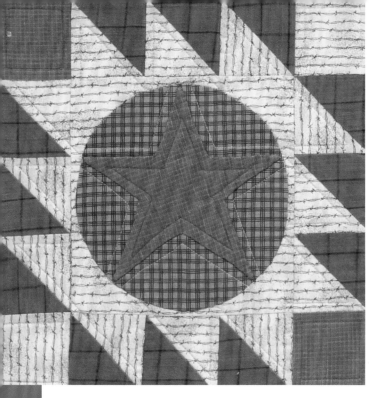

Making the Border Units

Sew a red 3" square to a blue-gray 3" × 8" rectangle. Make 16 units. Sew a dark blue 3" square to the opposite end of 10 of the rectangles. Sew a light 3" square to the opposite end of the remaining six units.

Make 10.   Make 6.

Assembling the Quilt

1 Arrange the blocks in five rows of three blocks each, alternating the Star blocks with the Four Patch blocks. Position the border units at the end of each row, taking care to position the red, blue, or light squares according to the quilt assembly diagram.

2 For the top and bottom rows, arrange the remaining border units, referring to the diagram. Place a red 3" square in the top-left and bottom-right corners; position a light 3" square in the two remaining corners.

Quilt assembly

Making the Four Patch Blocks

1 Using two matching red 4¼" squares and two matching dark blue 4¼" squares, sew the squares together to make a four-patch unit as shown.

2 Select four matching light 3" × 8" rectangles. Sew one to the left side and one to the right side of the four-patch unit. To the remaining two rectangles, sew a red 3" square to one end and a dark blue 3" square to the other end; make two matching units. Sew these units to the top and bottom of the four-patch unit. The block should measure 13"square, including seam allowances. Make seven blocks.

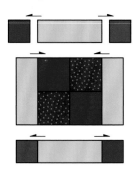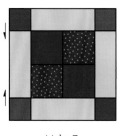

Make 7.

3 When you're pleased with the arrangement, sew the rows together. Join the rows. Press the seam allowances in one direction.

Finishing the Quilt

For detailed instructions on any of the finishing steps, go to ShopMartingale.com/HowtoQuilt for free information.

1 Layer the backing, batting, and quilt top; baste.

2 Quilt by hand or machine. The quilt shown is outline quilted to echo the pieced shapes.

3 Join the 2¼"-wide blue plaid binding strips end to end to make double-fold binding; attach it to the quilt.

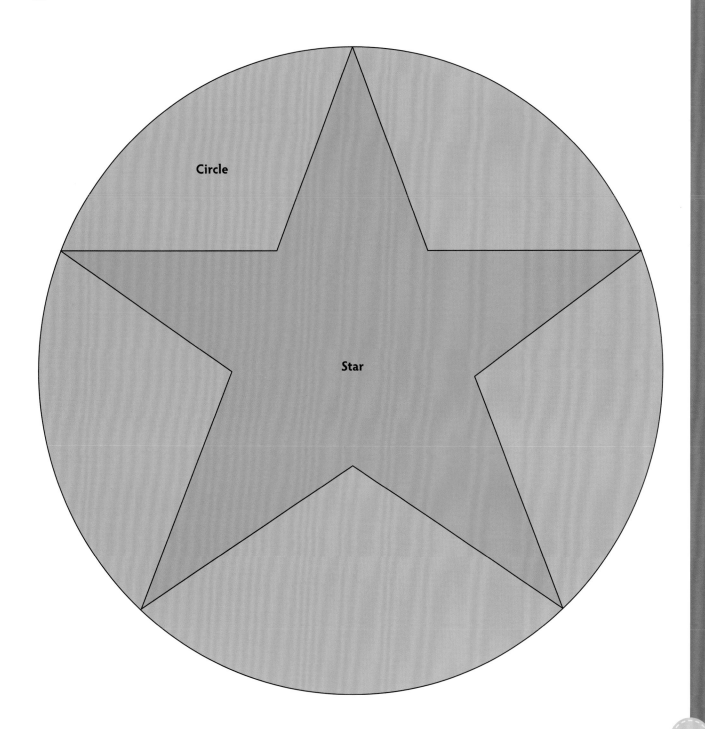

Circle

Star

Finished quilt: 61" × 75½"
Finished block: 3½" × 7½"

*Designed and pieced by Leanne Clare;
quilted by Karen M. Burns*

Emerald Forest

LEANNE CLARE

Leanne found a fat-quarter collection of beautiful Asian prints and fell in love with it. The lovely shades of greens reminded her of a forest. She added a brown batik to pull them all together and create an aura of depth and lushness.

Materials

Yardage is based on 42"-wide fabric. Fat quarters are 18" × 21".

8 coordinating Asian print fat quarters (see "Stash Option" at right)

4⅛ yards of brown batik for sashing and inner and outer borders

⅜ yard of light green fabric for middle border

⅔ yard of dark brown batik for binding

4⅝ yards of fabric for backing

67" × 82" piece of batting

Cutting

From *each* of the 8 fat quarters, cut:

10 rectangles, 4" × 8" (80 total; 3 are extra)

From the brown batik, cut:

5 strips, 4" × 42"; crosscut into:
    11 squares, 4" × 4"
    66 rectangles, 2" × 4"

7 strips, 3" × 42"

19 strips, 2¼" × 42"; crosscut into 308 squares, 2¼" × 2¼"

24 strips, 2" × 42"

From the light green fabric, cut:

7 strips, 1½" × 42"

From the dark brown batik, cut:

8 binding strips, 2½" × 42"

Stash Option

If you would like to whittle down your pile of scraps instead of using fat quarters for this quilt, you'll need 77 rectangles, 4" × 8", of assorted prints.

Assembling the Quilt Top

After sewing each seam, press seam allowances in the directions indicated by the arrows.

1. Using a 4" × 8" rectangle and four 2¼" brown batik squares, sew a square to each corner, referring to "Folded Corners" on page 57. Make 77.

Make 77.

2. Piece together 17 of the 2" brown batik strips to form one long strip. Cut into 10 vertical sashing strips, 65½" long.

Sew the blocks, rectangles, and squares to make the vertical rows. Press the seam allowances toward the sashing rectangles and squares. Sew the rows together with the vertical sashing strips; press the seam allowances toward the vertical sashing.

Assembling the Quilt Top

1 Measure the width of the quilt through the center. Sew the remaining 2"-wide brown strips together end to end to make one long length. Cut two strips for the top and bottom and sew them to the quilt. Press all seam allowances away from the center. Measure the length of the quilt through the center, cut two brown strips, and add them to the sides. Press.

2 For the middle border, measure the quilt, and then piece and add the 1½" green strips as you did for the inner border.

3 Repeat to add the 3"-wide brown strips for the outer border.

Finishing the Quilt

For detailed instructions on any of the finishing steps, go to ShopMartingale.com/HowtoQuilt for free information.

1 Layer the backing, batting, and quilt top; baste.

2 Quilt by hand or machine. The quilt shown is quilted with a pattern of leaves and vines.

3 Use the dark brown 2½"-wide strips to make the binding; attach it to the quilt.

3 Arrange the blocks from step 1 in 11 vertical rows of seven blocks each, separated by 2" × 4" brown batik rectangles. Add a vertical sashing strip between each row and offset the blocks as shown by adding the 4" brown batik squares to the top or bottom of each row. Rearrange the blocks as desired until you're satisfied with the color placement.

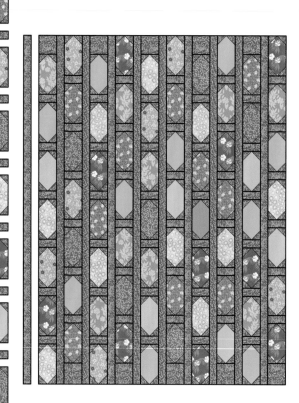

Folded Corners

When you're working exclusively with uniform-width strips, such as 2½"-wide Jelly Roll strips, making triangle shapes that finish to the same dimensions as square or rectangular pieces won't work if you cut them traditionally. But if you use one of the cleverest tricks around—the folded corner—you can make accurate 45° angles that work perfectly without having to cut triangles.

If you're not familiar with the folded-corner technique, here's how to do it. This example shows a rectangle with contrasting corners, but you can also use the technique for strips and squares.

1 Draw a diagonal line from corner to corner on the wrong side of a 2¼" square (or other size as specified in the project directions).

2 Position the square right sides together on the corner of the rectangle as shown, so that the diagonal line goes from the top edge to the side edge, not from the corner to the interior of the rectangle.

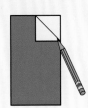

3 Stitch on the marked line. Press to set the stitches, and then trim away the excess fabric in the corner, leaving a ¼"-wide seam allowance. Press the remaining triangle of fabric open.

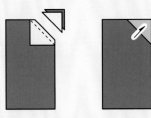

4 Continue as described in your project's instructions, using the folded-corner technique to either add squares to the remaining corners of the rectangle or to add squares to the ends of strips.

Scrappy Squares

CHERYL WALL

This pattern combines a strong, symmetrical design with typical country colors and motifs. Is the quilt primitive or formal, country or urban? You decide!

Materials

Yardage is based on 42"-wide fabric.

1⅓ yards of dark blue fabric for blocks, inner border, tulip centers, and large hearts

⅓ yard each of 12 different medium fabrics for blocks

⅔ yard of muslin or other light fabric for blocks

1⅜ yards of green-striped fabric for outer border

½ yard of green fabric for stems and leaves

⅓ yard of red fabric for tulips and small hearts

¼ yard of gold fabric for stars

⅝ yard of fabric for binding

3¾ yards of backing fabric

65" × 79" piece of batting

Fabric Hints

Keep the dark and light fabrics the same for each of the 12 blocks to create a consistent graphic design. Use a variety of medium fabrics for background interest.

Cutting

All measurements include ¼"-wide seam allowances.

From the dark blue fabric, cut:
22 strips, 1½" × 42"; crosscut *16* of the strips into:
    24 strips, 1½" × 10½"
    48 strips, 1½" × 6½"

From *each* of the 12 medium fabrics, cut:
2 squares, 2½" × 2½" (24 total)
4 rectangles, 2½" × 3½" (48 total)
1 rectangle, 2½" × 5½" (12 total)
1 strip, 2½" × 8½" (12 total)
1 strip, 2½" × 10½" (12 total)
1 rectangle, 3½" × 5½" (12 total)
1 rectangle, 5½" × 10½" (12 total)

From the muslin, cut:
12 strips, 1½" × 42"; crosscut *each* strip into:
    1 strip, 1½" × 10½" (12 total)
    1 strip, 1½" × 5½" (12 total)
    4 strips, 1½" × 4½" (48 total)
    2 rectangles, 1½" × 2½" (24 total)

From the green-striped fabric, cut:
6 strips, 7½" × 42"

From the green fabric, cut:
2 strips, 1½" × 31"
2 strips, 1½" × 42"

From the binding fabric, cut:
7 strips, 2¼" × 42"

Finished quilt: 58½" × 72½"

Finished block: 14" × 14"

*Pieced and appliquéd by Cheryl Wall;
machine quilted by Mary Flynn*

Making the Blocks

After sewing each seam, press seam allowances
in the directions indicated by the arrows.

1 Sew one dark 1½" × 10½" strip, one medium
2½" × 10½" strip, and one muslin 1½" × 10½"
strip together lengthwise as shown. Crosscut four
segments, 2½" wide.

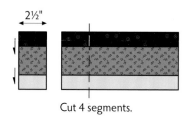

Cut 4 segments.

2 Sew one dark 1½" × 10½" strip and one medium
5½" × 10½" rectangle together lengthwise.
Crosscut four segments, 2½" wide.

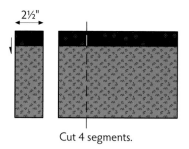

Cut 4 segments.

3 Sew one medium 3½" × 5½" strip, one muslin
1½" × 5½" strip, and one medium 2½" × 5½"
strip together lengthwise as shown. Crosscut two
segments, 2½" wide.

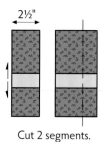

Cut 2 segments.

4 Sew two muslin 1½" × 2½" rectangles, two
medium 2½" squares, and one medium
2½" × 8½" strip together as shown.

5 Sew a muslin 1½" × 4½" strip to the left side of
a segment from step 1 as shown. Sew a medium
2½" × 3½" rectangle to the top of the unit. Sew a dark
1½" × 6½" strip to the right side of the unit.

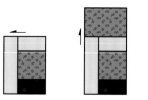

6 Sew a pieced segment from step 2 to the left side of the unit as shown.

7 Repeat steps 5 and 6 to make four pieced squares.

8 Sew one segment from step 3 between two pieced squares as shown. Make two.

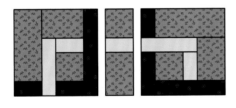

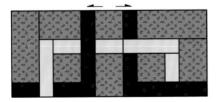

Make 2.

9 Sew the pieced strip from step 4 between the two units from step 8 to complete the block. Repeat steps 1–9 to make 12 blocks that measure 14½" square, including seam allowances.

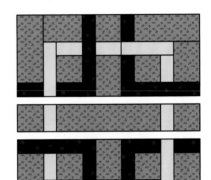

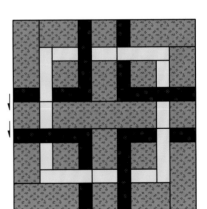

Assembling the Quilt Top

1 Arrange the blocks in four rows of three blocks each. Sew the blocks in each row together, and then sew the rows together. The quilt top should measure 42½" × 56½", including seam allowances.

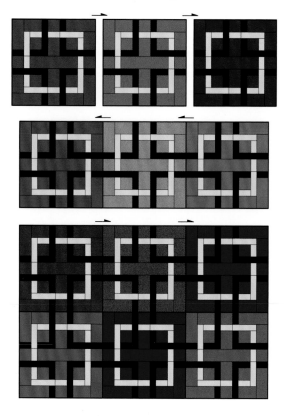

2 Sew the six remaining dark blue 1½" × 42" strips together end to end. Cut two strips, 44½" long, and two strips, 56½" long. Sew the 56½"-long strips to the sides of the quilt top. Sew the 44½"-long strips to the top and bottom edges of the quilt top. The quilt top should measure 44½" × 58½", including seam allowances.

3 Sew the green 7½" × 42" outer-border strips together end to end. Cut four strips, 58½" long. Sew the strips to the sides of the quilt top. Sew the two remaining strips to the top and bottom edges of the quilt top.

Adding the Appliqués

1 Using the dark blue, green, red, and gold fabrics and the patterns on page 63, cut out the appliqué shapes. Make the quantity indicated on the pattern for each shape. Fold each of the green 1½" × 31" strips and 1½" × 42" strips in half lengthwise, wrong sides together, and sew a scant ¼" from the raw edges. Center the seam allowances on the back of the strips and press to one side. Center the shorter strips on the top and bottom outer borders and the longer strips on the side outer borders. Pin in place.

2 Using the photo on page 60 as a guide for placement, arrange 12 leaves on each of the side stems and 8 leaves on the top and bottom stems. Pin in place.

3 Pin the hearts, tulips, and stars in place.

4 Appliqué all pieces in place.

Finishing the Quilt

For detailed instructions on any of the finishing steps, go to ShopMartingale.com/HowtoQuilt for free information.

1 Layer the backing, batting, and quilt top; baste.

2 Quilt by hand or machine. The quilt shown is quilted with petals in the blocks and corners and with outline quilting and swirls in the border.

3 Use the 2¼"-wide strips to make the double-fold binding; attach it to the quilt.

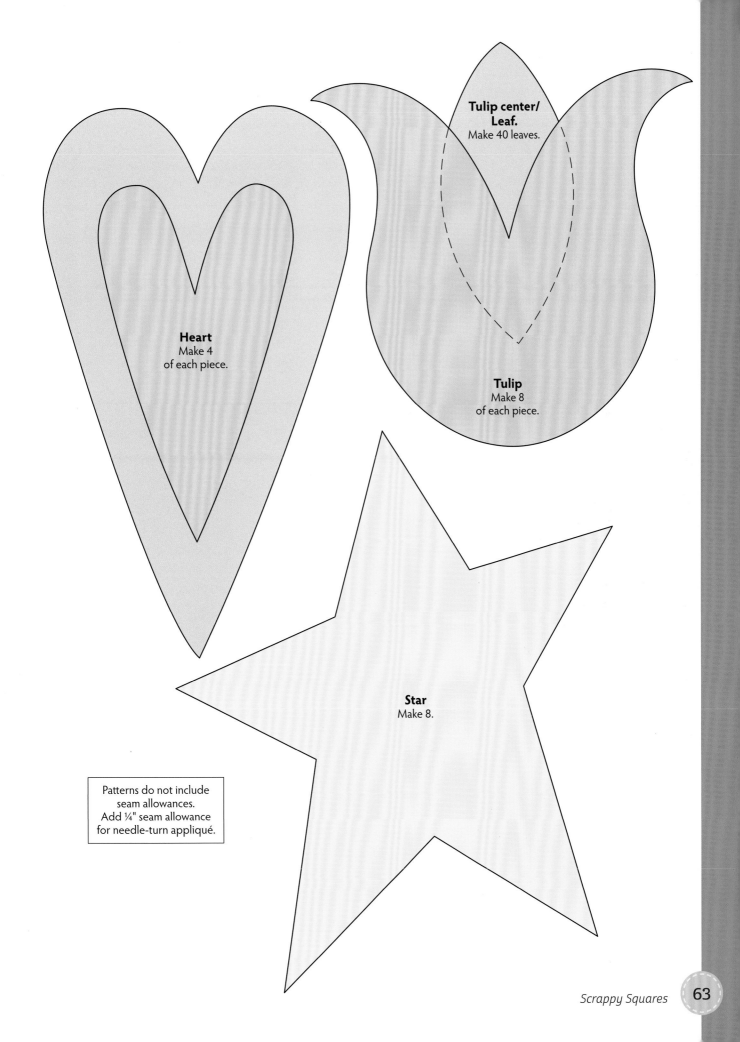

**Tulip center/
Leaf.**
Make 40 leaves.

Heart
Make 4
of each piece.

Tulip
Make 8
of each piece.

Star
Make 8.

Patterns do not include
seam allowances.
Add ¼" seam allowance
for needle-turn appliqué.

Snowflakes

JENNY WILDING CARDON

Combine easy blocks and quick raw-edge appliqué in this cute quilt, which will ward off the winter chill—and keep you cozy from first snowfall to last! The quiltmaker, Jenny Wilding Cardon, used Aspen Frost fabrics by Basic Grey for Moda.

Materials

Yardage is based on 42"-wide fabric.

1⅞ yards of white-on-white print for blocks and appliqués

2⅞ yards of light blue snowflake print for blocks and binding

1¼ yards of turquoise print for blocks and binding

3¾ yards of fabric for backing

61" × 70" piece of batting

Washable glue stick

Quarter or other medium-sized coin

Cutting

All measurements include ¼"-wide seam allowances.

From the white-on-white print, cut:
72 squares, 5" × 5"
Reserve the remaining white print for appliqués.

From the light blue snowflake print, cut:
28 squares, 10" × 10"
3 squares, 9½" × 9½"
12 strips, 2" × 12½"

From the turquoise print, cut:
8 squares, 10" × 10"
3 squares, 9½" × 9½"
12 strips, 2" × 12½"

Making the Pieced Blocks

After sewing each seam, press seam allowances in the directions indicated by the arrows.

1 Draw a diagonal line from corner to corner on the wrong side of each white 5" square. Place a marked square on one corner of a light blue 10" square, right sides together and raw edges aligned. Sew on the marked line. Trim the excess corner fabric, leaving a ¼" seam allowance. Flip the corner triangle open. Repeat on the opposite corner of the blue square to complete one pieced square. Make 28.

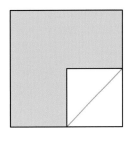 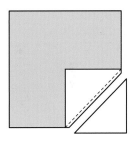

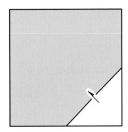 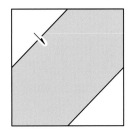

Make 28.

Finished quilt: 54½" × 63½"

Finished block: 9" × 9"

triangles and the turquoise/white triangles to make a total of eight blue/turquoise pieced blocks. Trim all 36 blocks to measure 9½" square.

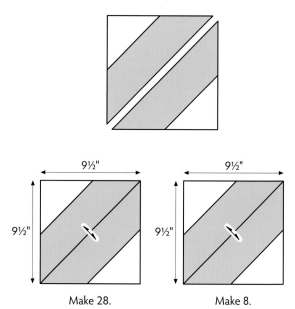

Make 28.   Make 8.

Making the Snowflake Blocks

1 Trace the snowflake pattern (page 67) onto cardstock—a bright light or window behind the template makes this easier—and cut it out. Trace 36 snowflake shapes onto the wrong side of the remaining white print, leaving at least ½" of space between the shapes. Cut out the shapes just inside the drawn lines.

2 In the same manner, use 16 white squares and eight turquoise 10" squares to make eight pieced squares.

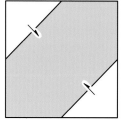

Make 8.

3 Cut the 36 pieced squares made in steps 1 and 2 in half diagonally to yield 72 pieced triangles. Sew two light blue/white triangles together along their long edges to make one blue/white pieced block. Press the seam allowances open to reduce bulk. Repeat to make a total of 28 blue/white pieced blocks. In the same manner, use the remaining blue/white

2 Fold a light blue 9½" square in half vertically and horizontally to find the center point. Place a quarter over the center point, dabbing a bit of the glue stick on the coin to keep it in place. Position six snowflake appliqués evenly spaced around the quarter, so that their tips are just touching the edge of the quarter. Dab the appliqués with a tiny bit of the glue stick to keep them in place for raw-edge machine appliqué. Remove the quarter.

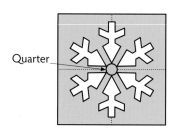

Quarter

3 Using white thread, topstitch a scant ¼" from the raw edges of the appliqués to secure them. When you reach the tip of each snowflake appliqué, stitch to the point, backstitch, and then continue around the shape as before.

4 Repeat steps 2–4 to make a total of three Snowflake blocks with light blue backgrounds and three Snowflake blocks with turquoise backgrounds.

Make 3.   Make 3.

Assembling the Quilt Top

Using the quilt photo as a guide, lay out the blocks in seven rows of six blocks each. Sew the blocks into rows and press the seam allowances in opposite directions from row to row. Sew the rows together and press the seam allowances in one direction.

Finishing the Quilt

For detailed instructions on any of the finishing steps, go to ShopMartingale.com/HowtoQuilt for free information.

1 Layer the backing, batting, and quilt top; baste.

2 Quilt by hand or machine. The quilt shown is quilted with an allover pattern of swirls and wavy lines.

3 Alternating colors, join the light blue and turquoise 12½"-long strips by layering the strips, right sides together, at a right angle and sewing across the diagonal as shown. Trim ¼" from the stitching line and press the seam allowances open. Attach the binding to the quilt.

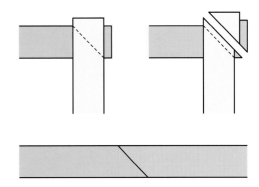

4 Using laundry detergent and fabric softener, run your finished quilt through a normal cycle in your washer and dryer to fray the raw edges of the snowflake appliqués. If needed after drying, trim away any long threads.

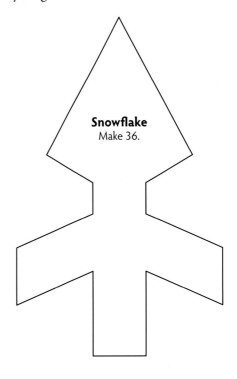

Snowflake
Make 36.

Pattern does not include
seam allowance.

Finished quilt: 59" × 77"

Finished block: 13½" × 13½"

Counted Nine Patch

SHERRI FALLS

Make double Nine Patch blocks on the double by building them from smaller nine-patch units. Add pink-and-white cornerstones to create Nine Patch blocks in the sashing for a delightful, unifying touch that gives the quilt the look of counted cross-stitch.

Materials

Yardage is based on 42"-wide fabric.
Fat eighths are 9" × 21".

4 yards of white solid for blocks and sashing
12 fat eighths *total* of assorted blue, green, and pink prints for blocks
⅜ yard of pink tone on tone for blocks and sashing
⅔ yard of blue print for binding
5 yards of fabric for backing
66" × 83" piece of batting

Cutting

All measurements include ¼"-wide seam allowances.

From the white solid, cut:
4 strips, 14" × 42"; crosscut into 31 strips, 5" × 14"
6 strips, 5" × 42"; crosscut into 48 squares, 5" × 5"
22 strips, 2" × 42"; crosscut 15 of the strips into:
    12 strips, 2" × 21"
    24 strips, 2" × 10"
    24 rectangles, 2" × 5"

From *each* of the assorted blue, green, and pink prints, cut:
2 strips, 2" × 21" (24 total)
1 strip, 2" × 10" (12 total)

From the pink tone on tone, cut:
5 strips, 2" × 42"

From the blue print, cut:
8 strips, 2½" × 42"

Making the Blocks

After sewing each seam, press seam allowances in the directions indicated by the arrows.

1 Sew a white 2" × 21" strip between two matching print 2" × 21" strips as shown. Crosscut the strip set into eight segments, 2" wide.

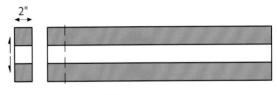

Make 1 strip set.
Cut 8 segments.

2 Using a print that matches the print in step 1, sew a 2" × 10" strip between two white 2" × 10" strips as shown. Crosscut the strip set into four segments, 2" wide.

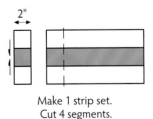

Make 1 strip set.
Cut 4 segments.

3 Arrange two segments from step 1 and one
segment from step 2 as shown. Join the
segments. Make four identical nine-patch units that
measure 5" square, including seam allowances.

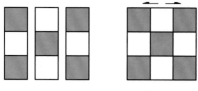

Make 4.

4 Repeat steps 1–3 with the remaining print strips
to make a total of 48 nine-patch units.

5 Sew a white 2" × 42" strip between two pink
2" × 42" strips as shown. Crosscut the strip set
into 20 segments, 2" wide.

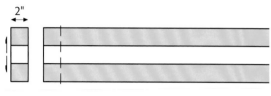

Make 1 strip set.
Cut 20 segments.

6 Sew a pink 2" × 42" strip between two white
2" × 42" strips as shown. Make three strip sets.
From the strip sets, cut 52 segments, 2" wide.

Make 3 strip sets.
Cut 52 segments.

7 Join one segment from step 5 and two segments
from step 6 to make a sashing block as shown.
Make 20 sashing blocks that measure 5" square,
including seam allowances.

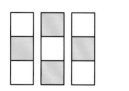

Make 20.

8 Sew one of the remaining segments from
step 6 between two white 2" × 5" rectangles as
shown to make a block center. Make 12 units that
measure 5" square, including seam allowances.

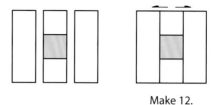

Make 12.

9 Arrange four white 5" squares, four matching
nine-patch units, and one block center in three
rows as shown. Join the units in each row. Join the
rows. Make one block from each print for a total of
12 blocks that measure 14" square, including seam
allowances.

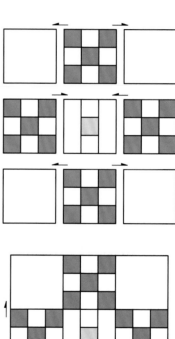

Make 12.

Assembling the Quilt Top

1 Arrange three blocks and four white 5" × 14" sashing strips in a row as shown. Join the blocks and strips. Make four rows.

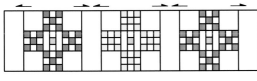

Make 4.

2 Join three white 5" × 14" sashing strips and four sashing blocks as shown. Make five sashing rows.

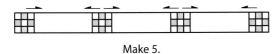

Make 5.

3 Lay out the block and sashing rows as shown in the quilt assembly diagram. Join the rows.

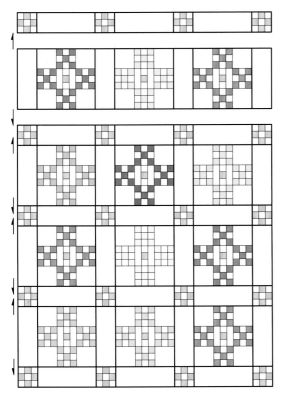

Quilt assembly

Finishing the Quilt

For detailed instructions on any of the finishing steps, go to ShopMartingale.com/HowtoQuilt for free information.

1 Layer the backing, batting, and quilt top; baste.

2 Quilt by hand or machine. The quilt shown is quilted with allover swirl design.

3 Use the blue 2½"-wide strips to make the binding; attach it to the quilt.

Ohio Star Crossing

CONNIE TESENE AND MARY ETHERINGTON FOR COUNTRY THREADS

Featuring classic blocks in use during the Civil War, Ohio Star Crossing is named for a state drawn into the push and pull of those times. The northern portion of Ohio supplied much-needed troops and cash to the Union army, while southern Ohio's alliances leaned more toward the Confederacy. Two minor battles took place in Ohio, and a camp near Sandusky by Lake Erie housed Confederate prisoners of war.

Materials

Yardage is based on 42"-wide fabric.

½ yard *total* of assorted scraps in cream and ivory prints for Ohio Star blocks

1 yard *total* of assorted scraps in dark blue, red, brown, and black prints for Ohio Star and Checkerboard blocks

½ yard *total* of assorted scraps in medium gray, tan, brown, and blue prints for Ohio Star blocks

½ yard *total* of assorted scraps in light cream, red, tan, and taupe prints for Checkerboard blocks

¼ yard *each* of 6 assorted light prints for spacer blocks

½ yard of dark print for bias binding

2¾ yards of fabric for backing (pieced horizontally)

49" × 61" piece of batting

Cutting

All measurements include ¼"-wide seam allowances.

From the assorted scraps of cream and ivory prints, cut:

18 sets of 2 matching squares, 3¼" × 3¼" (36 total); cut the squares into quarters diagonally to yield 18 sets of 8 matching triangles (144 total)

From the assorted scraps of dark blue, red, brown, and black prints, cut:

18 sets of 2 matching squares, 3¼" × 3¼" (36 total); cut the squares into quarters diagonally to yield 18 sets of 8 matching triangles (144 total)

18 squares, 2½" × 2½"

252 squares, 1½" × 1½"

From the assorted scraps of medium gray, tan, brown, and blue prints, cut:

18 sets of 4 matching squares, 2½" × 2½" (72 total)

From the assorted scraps of light cream, red, tan, and taupe prints, cut:

252 squares, 1½" × 1½"

From the 6 assorted ¼-yard light prints, cut:

31 squares, 6½" × 6½"

From the dark print, cut:

2¼"-wide bias strips, enough to yield 200" of binding

Making the Ohio Star Blocks

You can use one light, one medium, and one dark print for each block, or mix some of them up to get the same look as this quilt. After sewing each seam, press seam allowances in the directions indicated by the arrows.

1. Join two cream or ivory 3¼" triangles and two dark 3¼" triangles. Make four units.

Make 4.

73

Finished quilt: 42½" × 54½"

Ohio Star block: 6" × 6"

Checkerboard block: 6" × 6"

Making the Checkerboard Blocks

1. Arrange 18 light 1½" squares and 18 dark 1½" squares into six rows of six squares each, alternating light and dark squares from row to row, and using the same print in each diagonal row.

2. Sew the squares together. Join the rows. The block should measure 6½" square, including seam allowances. Make 14 blocks.

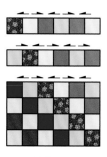

Make 14.

Assembling the Quilt Top

1. Arrange the Ohio Star blocks, Checkerboard blocks, and spacer blocks into nine rows, placing the Ohio Star blocks in the center and the Checkerboard blocks around the outside. Sew the blocks in rows. Join the rows.

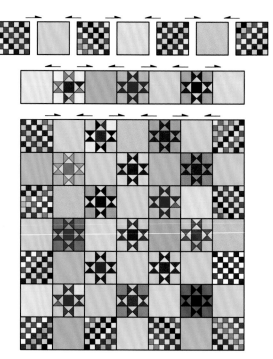

Quilt assembly

2. Join the four units from step 1, four medium 2½" squares, and one dark 2½" square. The block should measure 6½" square, including seam allowances. Make 18 blocks.

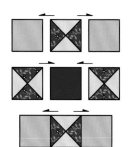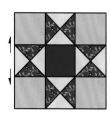

Make 18.

2 You can leave the quilt top square, or round the corners as we did. Place a 5"-diameter plate or cardboard circle on the corner block and trace the curve. Trim the corner on the drawn line.

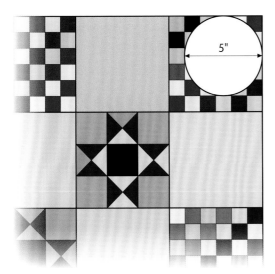

Finishing the Quilt

For detailed instructions on any of the finishing steps, go to ShopMartingale.com/HowtoQuilt for free information.

1 Layer the backing, batting, and quilt top; baste.

2 Quilt by hand or machine. The quilt shown is quilted with an allover meander pattern.

3 Use the blue 2¼"-wide bias-binding strips to make the binding; attach it to the quilt.

Finished quilt: 59½" × 70½"

Finished block: 11" × 11"

Designed by Kimberly Jolly; pieced by Codi Mangrum;
quilted by Diane Selman of MyLongArm.com

Sprightly Stars

KIMBERLY JOLLY

Turn your stash into stars! Start by choosing 10 fat quarters, then set your sights on making a star attraction.

Materials

Yardage is based on 42"-wide fabric. Fat quarters are 18" × 21".

10 fat quarters of assorted bright prints for blocks
1⅜ yards of navy stripe for blocks, middle border, and binding
2¾ yards of white dot for blocks and inner border
1⅞ yards of multicolored print for outer border
3¾ yards of fabric for backing
66" × 77" piece of batting

Cutting

All measurements include ¼"-wide seam allowances.

From *each* of the 10 bright print fat quarters, cut:
1 square, 4⅞" × 4⅞" (10 total)
16 squares, 2½" × 2½" (160 total)
8 squares, 2" × 2" (80 total)

From the navy stripe, cut:
8 strips, 2½" × 42"
10 squares, 4⅞" × 4⅞"
4 strips, 1¾" × 42"; crosscut into 80 squares, 1¾" × 1¾"
6 strips, 1½" × 42"

From the white dot, cut:
14 strips, 2½" × 42"; crosscut into:
    80 rectangles, 2½" × 4½"
    80 squares, 2½" × 2½"
6 strips, 2" × 42"
80 strips, 2" × 8½"

From the *lengthwise* grain of the multicolored print, cut:
2 strips, 5½" × 60½"
2 strips, 5½" × 59½"

Making the Blocks

After sewing each seam, press seam allowances in the directions indicated by the arrows.

1 Draw a diagonal line from corner to corner on the wrong side of the bright 4⅞" squares. Place one marked square and one navy 4⅞" square with right sides together. Sew ¼" from each side of the marked line. Cut the squares apart on the marked line to yield two half-square-triangle units that measure 4½" square, including seam allowances. Repeat to make 20 units.

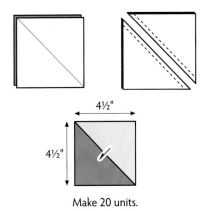

Make 20 units.

2 Draw a diagonal line from corner to corner on the wrong side of two matching bright 2½" squares. Place a marked square on one end of a white rectangle with right sides together, orienting the line as shown. Stitch on the marked line, and then trim the seam allowance to ¼". Repeat to add a matching bright square to the opposite end of the rectangle. The flying-geese unit should measure 2½" × 4½", including seam allowances. Make four.

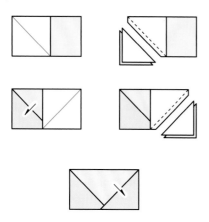

3 Draw a diagonal line from corner to corner on the wrong side of the navy 1¾" squares. Place a marked square on the bottom-right corner of the flying-geese unit with right sides together as shown. Stitch on the marked line, and then trim the seam allowance to ¼". Repeat to make four matching units that measure 2½" × 4½", including seam allowances.

Make 4 units,
2½" × 4½".

4 Lay out four white 2½" squares, the four matching flying-geese units, and a matching half-square-triangle unit in three rows as shown. Join the units in each row, and then join the rows. The block center should measure 8½" square, including seam allowances.

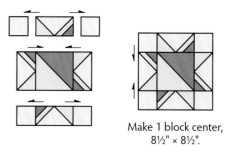

Make 1 block center,
8½" × 8½".

5 Lay out four matching bright 2" squares, four white 2" × 8½" strips, and the block center in three rows. Join the units in each row, and then join the rows. The Sprightly Star block should measure 11½" square, including seam allowances. Repeat to make 20 blocks.

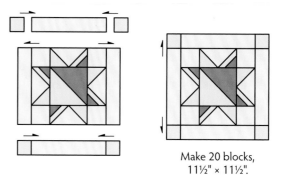

Make 20 blocks,
11½" × 11½".

Assembling the Quilt Top

1 Lay out the blocks in five rows of four, rotating them as shown in the quilt assembly diagram at right. Join the blocks in each row, and then join the rows. The quilt center should measure 44½" × 55½", including seam allowances.

2 Join the white 2"-wide strips end to end. From the pieced length, cut two strips, 55½" long, for the side borders and two strips, 47½" long, for the top and bottom borders. Sew the side borders to the quilt top first, and then add the top and bottom borders. The quilt top should measure 47½" × 58½", including seam allowances.

3 Join the navy 1½"-wide strips end to end. From the pieced length, cut two strips, 58½" long, for the side borders and two strips, 49½" long, for the top and bottom borders. Sew the side borders to the quilt top first, and then add the top and bottom borders. The quilt top should now measure 49½" × 60½", including seam allowances.

4 Sew the multicolored 60½"-long strips to the sides of the quilt center, and then add the multicolored 59½"-long strips to the top and bottom. The finished quilt top should measure 59½" × 70½".

Finishing the Quilt

For detailed instructions on any of the finishing steps, go to ShopMartingale.com/HowtoQuilt for free information.

1 Layer the backing, batting, and quilt top; baste.

2 Quilt by hand or machine. The quilt shown is quilted with allover circle pattern.

3 Use the navy stripe 2½"-wide strips to make the binding; attach it to the quilt.

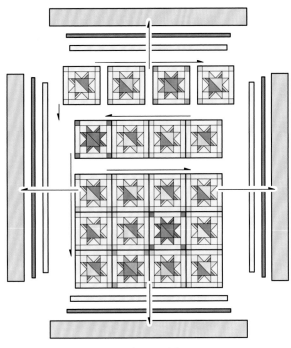

Quilt assembly

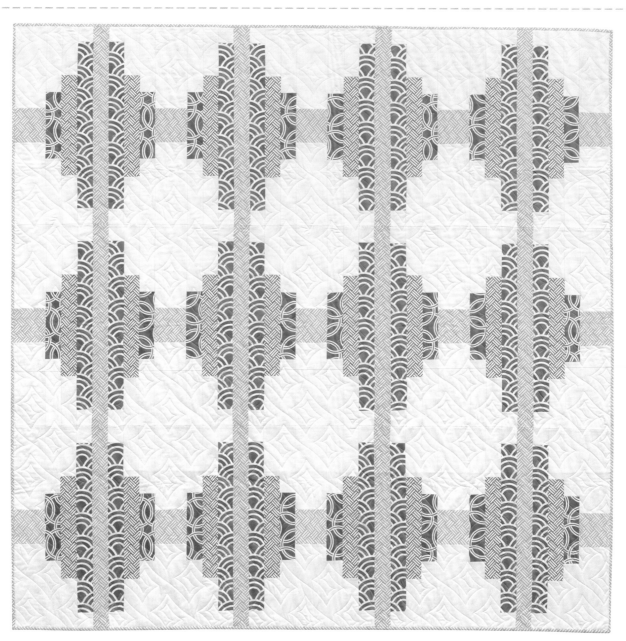

Finished quilt: 76½" × 72½"

Finished block: 14" × 24"

Pieced and machine quilted by Linda Barrett

Connections

SUSAN GUZMAN

Artful fabric inspired this design. The simple, clean blocks are refreshing against the white background. Because the fabrics are simple two-color prints, the quilt design is uncomplicated as well.

Materials

Yardage is based on 42"-wide fabric.

3 yards of white solid for blocks and sashing
1⅜ yards of pink print #1 for blocks
⅞ yard of pink print #2 for blocks
⅝ yard of pink print #3 for blocks
1½ yards of green print for blocks and binding
5 yards of backing fabric
83" × 79" piece of batting

Color-Palette Change Up

Selecting two bold fabrics for prints #1 and #3 and a more subtle fabric for print #2 breaks up the intensity of the block design. If you prefer a darker color palette, choose three dark fabrics for the pink prints, a medium-value fabric for the green print, and a light small-scale print for the background.

Cutting

All measurements include ¼"-wide seam allowances.

From the white solid, cut:
3 strips, 2½" × 42"; crosscut into 48 squares,
    2½" × 2½" (A)
3 strips, 6½" × 42"; crosscut into 48 rectangles,
    2½" × 6½" (C)
3 strips, 8½" × 42"; crosscut into 48 rectangles,
    2½" × 8½" (E)
4 strips, 10½" × 42"; crosscut into 30 rectangles,
    4½" × 10½" (G)

From pink print #1, cut:
2 strips, 20½" × 42"; crosscut into 24 rectangles,
    2½" × 20½" (B)

From pink print #2, cut:
2 strips, 12½" × 42"; crosscut into 24 rectangles,
    2½" × 12½" (D)

From pink print #3, cut:
2 strips, 8½" × 42"; crosscut into 24 rectangles,
    2½" × 8½" (E)

From the green print, cut:
1 strip, 24½" × 42"; crosscut into:
    12 rectangles, 2½" × 24½" (F)
    10 squares, 4½" × 4½" (H)
1 strip, 4½" × 42"; crosscut into 5 squares,
    4½" × 4½" (H)
8 strips, 2¼" × 42"

Making the Blocks

After sewing each seam, press seam allowances in the directions indicated by the arrows.

1 Sew together two white A squares and one pink #1 B rectangle to make a 24½"-long pieced strip. Make a total of 24 pieced strips.

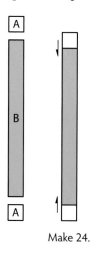

Make 24.

2 Sew together two white C rectangles and one pink #2 D rectangle to make a 24½"-long pieced strip. Make a total of 24 pieced strips.

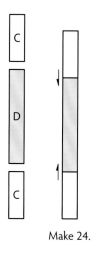

Make 24.

3 Sew together two white E rectangles and one pink #3 E rectangle to make a 24½"-long pieced strip. Make a total of 24 pieced strips.

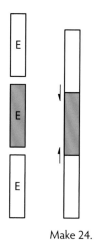

Make 24.

4 Lay out two strips from step 1, two strips from step 2, two strips from step 3, and one green F rectangle. Join the pieces to make one block that measures 14½" × 24½", including seam allowances. Make a total of 12 blocks.

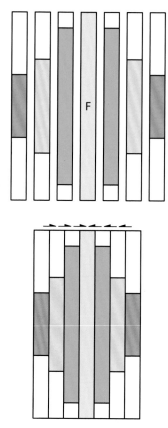

Make 12.

Assembling the Quilt Top

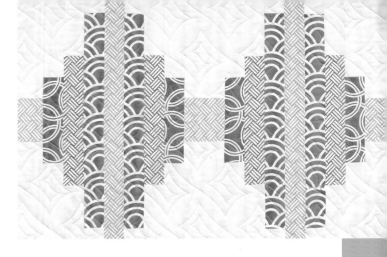

1 Join two white G rectangles and one green H square to make a sashing unit. Make a total of 15 units.

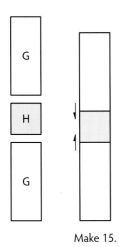

Make 15.

2 Lay out the blocks and sashing units in three rows, alternating the blocks and sashing units as shown in the quilt assembly diagram below. Sew the pieces together into rows. Sew the rows together to complete the quilt top.

Finishing the Quilt

For detailed instructions on any of the finishing steps, go to ShopMartingale.com/HowtoQuilt for free information.

1 Layer the backing, batting, and quilt top; baste.

2 Quilt by hand or machine. The quilt shown is quilted with a rectangular spiral pattern.

3 Use the green print 2½"-wide strips to make the binding; attach it to the quilt.

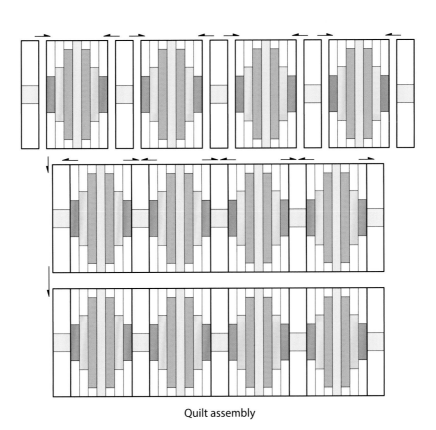

Quilt assembly

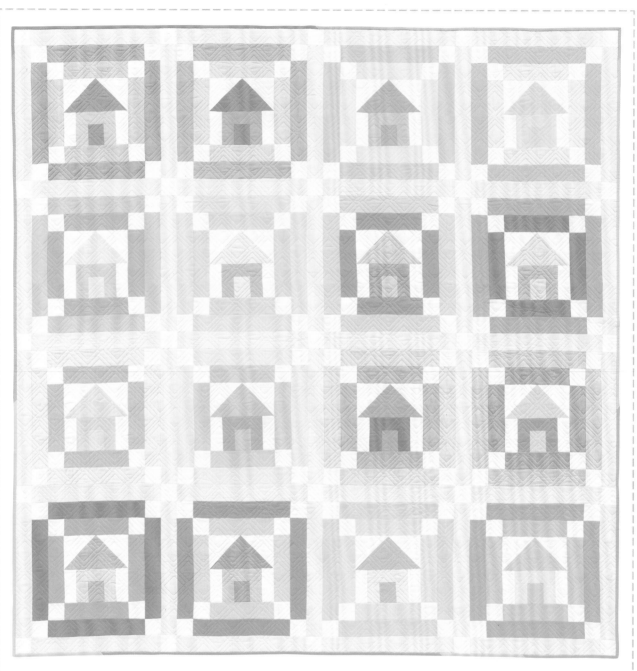

Finished quilt: 74½" × 74½"

Finished block: 16" × 16"

Designed and pieced by Corey Yoder;
quilted by Kaylene Parry

COREY YODER

S olid fabrics in sherbet tones make for a sweet and cheerful neighborhood. Frame each simple House block with a coordinating double border for a pleasing finished look.

Materials

Yardage is based on 42"-wide fabric.

⅓ yard *each* of 1 dark and 1 light shade of 8 assorted pastel solids (16 shades total) for blocks and binding: green, pink, blue, taupe, orange, coral, mint, and yellow

1½ yards of white solid for background

1½ yards of cream solid for sashing

5 yards of fabric for backing

83" × 83" piece of batting

Cutting

All measurements include ¼"-wide seam allowances.

From *each* of the 16 assorted pastel solids, cut:

1 strip, 2½" × 42"; crosscut into 3 rectangles,
    2½" × 12½" (48 total)

1 strip, 2½" × 42"; crosscut into 4 rectangles,
    2½" × 8½" (64 total)

1 strip, 4½" × 42"; crosscut into:
    1 rectangle, 4½" × 8½" (16 total)
    1 rectangle, 2½" × 12½" (16 total)
    1 rectangle, 2½" × 3" (16 total)
    1 rectangle, 2" × 5½" (16 total)
    2 rectangles, 2" × 3" (32 total)

From the remainder of 8 of the pastel solids, cut:

1 strip, 2½" × 42", for scrappy binding

From the white solid, cut:

4 strips, 4½" × 42"; crosscut into 32 squares, 4½" × 4½"

2 strips, 4½" × 42"; crosscut into 32 rectangles,
    2" × 4½"

10 strips, 2½" × 42"; crosscut into 153 squares,
    2½" × 2½"

From the cream solid, cut:

20 strips, 2½" × 42"; crosscut into 40 rectangles,
    2½" × 16½"

Making the House Blocks

The quilt contains 16 House blocks: 2 made from each of the eight colors. Pair the light and dark shades of each color to make a pair of blocks—for example, the light green house has a dark green door and roof, and vice versa. After sewing each seam, press seam allowances in the directions indicated by the arrows.

1 Draw a diagonal line from corner to corner on the wrong side of the white 4½" squares. Place a marked square on one end of a dark green 4½" × 8½" rectangle with right sides together. Sew on the drawn line, and then trim ¼" from the seam.

 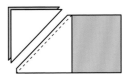

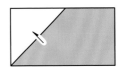

Make 16 units,
4½" × 8½".

2 Place a second white square on the opposite end of the rectangle, and then sew, trim, and press. This flying-geese unit is the roof section of the block. Repeat to make one roof from each solid for a total of 16 units. The units should measure 4½" × 8½.

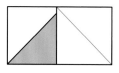
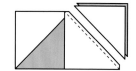
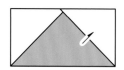

Make 16 units,
4½" × 8½".

3 Sew a light green 2" × 3" rectangle to each long side of the dark green 2½" × 3" rectangle. The unit should measure 3" × 5½". Sew a light green 2" × 5½" rectangle to the top of the unit. The unit should measure 4½" × 5½", including seam allowances.

Make 16 units,
4½" × 5½".

4 Sew white 2" × 4½" rectangles to the sides of the unit, which should now measure 4½" × 8½". Press toward the white rectangles. Sew the dark green roof to the top of the unit to complete the house. Make 16 blocks (two from each color pairing). The blocks should measure 8½" square, including seam allowances.

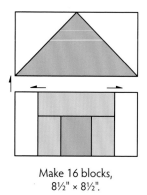

Make 16 blocks,
8½" × 8½".

Adding the Borders

Pair each of the House block colors with borders from a different color family. The four pairings shown are green/pink, blue/taupe, orange/coral, and mint/yellow. If the house has a light roof, use the dark shade for the inner border. If the house has a dark roof, use the light shade for the inner border. For example, for the house with the dark green roof, the inner border is light pink.

1 Sew light pink 2½" × 8½" rectangles to opposite sides of the House block with the dark green roof. The unit should measure 8½" × 12½", including seam allowances.

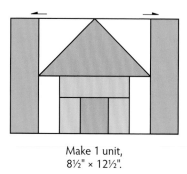

Make 1 unit,
8½" × 12½".

2 Sew a white 2½" square to each end of a light pink 2½" × 8½" rectangle. Repeat to make two pieced units that measure 2½" × 12½", including seam allowances.

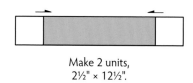

Make 2 units,
2½" × 12½".

3 Sew the units to the top and bottom of the block. The unit should measure 12½" square, including seam allowances.

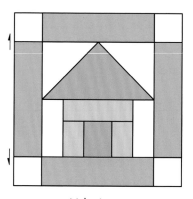

Make 1 unit,
12½" × 12½".

4 Sew dark pink 2½" × 12½" rectangles to opposite sides of the block. The unit should measure 12½" × 16½", including seam allowances.

6 Sew the units to the top and bottom of the block. The block should measure 16½" square, including seam allowances.

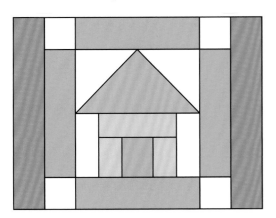

Make 1 unit,
12½" × 16½".

5 Sew a white 2½" square to each end of a dark pink 2½" × 12½" rectangle. Repeat to make two pieced units that measure 2½" × 16½", including seam allowances.

Make 2 units,
2½" × 16½".

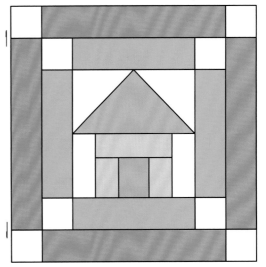

Make 1 block,
16½" × 16½".

7 Repeat steps 1–6 to make four blocks from each color pairing for a total of 16 blocks. For example, the pink/green color pairing yields four blocks as shown.

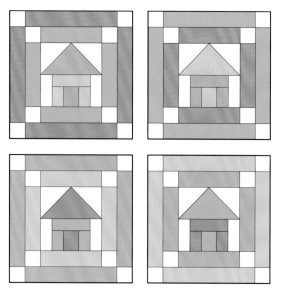

Each color pairing
will yield 4 blocks.

Assembling the Quilt Top

The quilt contains four block rows alternating with five sashing rows as shown in the quilt assembly diagram. For each block row, lay out four blocks alternating with five cream 2½" × 16½" strips. For each sashing row, lay out four cream 2½" × 16½" strips alternating with five white 2½" squares. Join the units in each row, and then join the rows.

Finishing the Quilt

For detailed instructions on any of the finishing steps, go to ShopMartingale.com/HowtoQuilt for free information.

1 Layer the backing, batting, and quilt top; baste.

2 Quilt by hand or machine. The quilt shown is quilted with an allover diagonal grid of squares.

3 Use the assorted pastel 2½"-wide strips to make scrappy binding; attach it to the quilt.

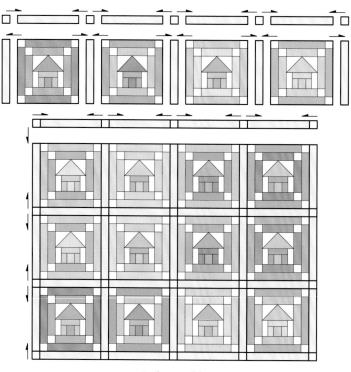

Quilt assembly

Hourglass Courthouse Steps

AUDRIE BIDWELL

Create a colorful hourglass pattern using the traditional Courthouse Steps block. Dive into your stash to incorporate a wide assortment of light and bright prints.

Materials

Yardage is based on 42"-wide fabric.

2⅞ yards *total* of assorted light prints for blocks

⅛ yard of black-and-white print for block centers

3¾ yards *total* of assorted medium to dark prints for blocks (collectively referred to as *dark*)*

⅔ yard of print for binding

4¾ yards of fabric for backing

74" × 85" piece of batting

*This is the equivalent of 84 strips, 1½" × 42"; 1 strip is enough to make 1 dark section of a block.

Cutting

All measurements include ¼"-wide seam allowances.

From the assorted light prints, cut a *total* of:
84 squares, 1½" × 1½"
84 logs, 1½" × 3½"
84 logs, 1½" × 5½"
84 logs, 1½" × 7½"
84 logs, 1½" × 9½"

From the black-and-white print, cut:
2 strips, 1½" × 42"; crosscut into 42 squares, 1½" × 1½"

From the assorted dark prints, cut *84 matching sets* of:
1 log, 1½" × 3½"
1 log, 1½" × 5½"
1 log, 1½" × 7½"
1 log, 1½" × 9½"
1 log, 1½" × 11½"

From the binding fabric, cut:
8 strips, 2½" × 42"

Finished quilt: 66½" × 77½"

Finished block: 11" × 11"

Designed and pieced by Audrie Bidwell;
quilted by Laura McCarrick

Making the Blocks

Each block has one black-and-white print center square, two dark sections with matching logs in each, and two light sections with scrappy logs in each. After sewing each seam, press all seam allowances away from the center square, toward the log just added, as indicated by the arrows.

1 Sew light 1½" squares to the top and bottom of the black-and-white center square. Sew a dark 1½" × 3½" log to each side of the center square.

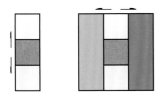

2 Sew light 1½" × 3½" logs to the top and bottom of the unit from step 1.

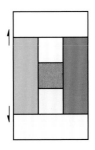

3 Sew matching dark 1½" × 5½" logs to the sides. Continue adding longer logs, alternating light and dark as shown to construct a block that is 11½" square, including seam allowances. Make 42 blocks.

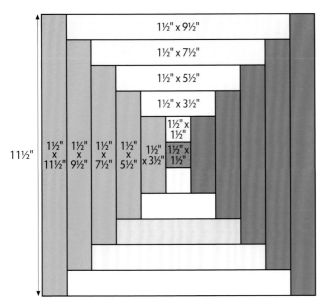

Make 42.

Assembling the Quilt Top

1 Arrange the blocks in seven horizontal rows of six blocks each, alternating the placement of the light and dark sections as shown in the quilt assembly diagram below.

2 Join the blocks in each row. Press the seam allowances in alternating directions from row to row. Join the rows.

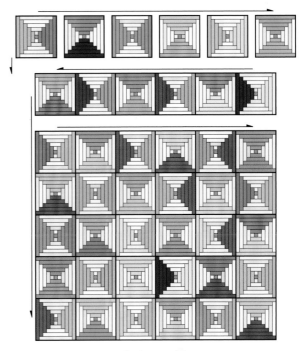

Quilt assembly

Finishing the Quilt

For detailed instructions on any of the finishing steps, go to ShopMartingale.com/HowtoQuilt for free information.

1 Layer the backing, batting, and quilt top; baste.

2 Quilt by hand or machine. The quilt shown is quilted with an allover loop design.

3 Use the 2½"-wide strips to make the binding; attach it to the quilt.

Garden Bramble

When Kim Diehl designs, she puts together groups of prints and colors that work well together but don't look as though they were created together. You can try this same scrappy approach to selecting fabrics. Try tossing the prints you're considering into a pile, take a step back, and look at the blend. When you love what you see, trust your instincts, grab a rotary cutter, and dive into the project.

Materials

Yardage is based on 42"-wide fabric. Fat quarters are 18" × 21" and fat eighths are 9" × 21".

1 fat quarter of green stripe or print for vines and leaves

10 fat quarters of assorted prints for blocks, berries, and border

1¾ yards of medium-light neutral print for blocks and border

½ yard of light-neutral print for blocks

¾ yard of dark blue print for flower centers and binding

½ yard of red print for flowers

2 fat eighths of assorted green prints for leaves

1 fat eighth of gold print for stars

3¼ yards of fabric for backing

56" × 66" piece of batting

Liquid fabric glue, water-soluble and acid-free

Cutting

All measurements include ¼"-wide seam allowances. Reserve scraps for appliqués.

From the green stripe or print, cut:
1½"-wide bias strips totaling at least 100" in length

From the assorted prints, cut a *total* of:
10 squares, 5⅞" × 5⅞"; cut the squares in half diagonally to yield 20 triangles

24 squares, 5½" × 5½"

26 squares, 3½" × 3½"

48 squares, 3" × 3"

From the medium-light neutral print, cut:
13 squares, 10½" × 10½"

10 squares, 5⅞" × 5⅞"; cut the squares in half diagonally to yield 20 triangles

From the light-neutral print, cut:
48 squares, 3" × 3"

From the dark blue print, cut:
6 strips, 2½" × 42"

Preparing the Appliqués

1 Using the patterns on pages 96 and 97, prepare 7 red flowers, 7 dark blue flower centers, 11 gold stars, 15 assorted-print berries, 11 assorted-green large leaves, 6 green-striped small leaves, and 9 assorted-green small leaves for your chosen appliqué method. The sample quilt uses the freezer-paper method and the invisible machine-appliqué technique found in designer Kim Diehl's books. For free, downloadable information on appliqué techniques, visit ShopMartingale.com/HowtoQuilt.

2 Using straight, not diagonal, seams, join the green bias strips to make four strips, 24" long. Press the seam allowances to one side, all in the same direction.

Finished quilt: 50½" × 60½"

Finished block: 10" × 10"

Designed, pieced, and machine appliquéd by Kim Diehl; machine quilted by Deborah Poole

Making Block A

Stitch all pieces with right sides together and a ¼" seam allowance unless otherwise noted. After sewing each seam, press seam allowances in the directions indicated by the arrows.

1 Draw a line from corner to corner on the wrong side of each assorted-print 3½" square. Place a marked square on one corner of a medium-light neutral 10½" square, right sides together and sew on the drawn line. Trim the excess corner fabric ¼" from the line.

2 Repeat step 1 to attach a second marked square to the opposite corner of the 10½"square. Make 13.

Make 13.

Making Block B

1 Sew an assorted-print 3" square to a light-neutral 3" square to make a two-patch unit. Make 48.

2 Sew the two-patch units together in pairs to make four-patch units. Make 24.

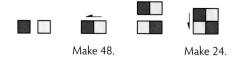

Make 48.   Make 24.

3 Arrange two four-patch units and two assorted-print 5½" squares as shown, noting the orientation of each four-patch unit. Sew the units in each row together. Join the rows to make block B, which should measure 10½" square, including seam allowances. Make 12.

3 Fold a 24"-long strip lengthwise, wrong sides together, and sew the long raw edges to make a tube. Press the tube flat, centering the seam allowances so they are not visible from the front of the stem. Apply small dots of liquid fabric glue every ½" under the seam allowances and use a hot, dry iron to heat set the seam allowances in place. Make four.

Block B.
Make 12.

Assembling the Quilt Top

1 Lay out the A and B blocks in an alternating arrangement, orienting the blocks as shown.

2 Sew the blocks together in rows. Join the rows to make the quilt top, which should measure 50½" square, including seam allowances.

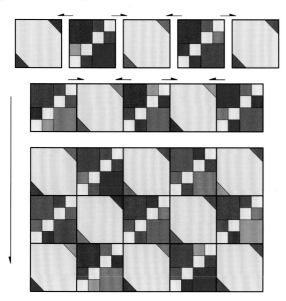

Quilt assembly

3 To add the borders, sew an assorted-print 5⅞" triangle to a medium-light neutral 5⅞" triangle along the long bias edge, being careful not to stretch the fabric. Trim away the dog-ear corners to square up the unit. Make 20.

Make 20.

4 Divide the half-square-triangle units into two groups, with one unit of each assorted print in each group. Sew 10 half-square-triangle units

together, orienting the units as shown, to make a top border. Make a second border, rotating the units as shown, for the bottom of the quilt.

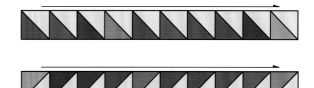

Make 1 of each.

5 Sew the borders to the top and bottom of the quilt.

Appliquéing the Quilt

1 Referring to the quilt photo on page 94 for placement, arrange the appliqués on the quilt top as shown.

2 Working in layers from the bottom to the top, glue baste the stems to the quilt top, and then pin or thread baste the remaining appliqués, ensuring that any raw fabric edges are overlapped by at least ¼". Stitch the appliqués in place.

Finishing the Quilt

For detailed instructions on any of the finishing steps, go to ShopMartingale.com/HowtoQuilt for free information.

1 Layer the backing, batting, and quilt top; baste.

2 Quilt by hand or machine. The quilt shown is quilted with small swirled circles filling the areas behind the appliqués and the patchwork blocks, with the appliqué designs shadow quilted in the open areas. The borders are quilted with straight lines to echo the triangles.

3 Use the dark blue 2½"-wide strips to make the binding; attach it to the quilt.

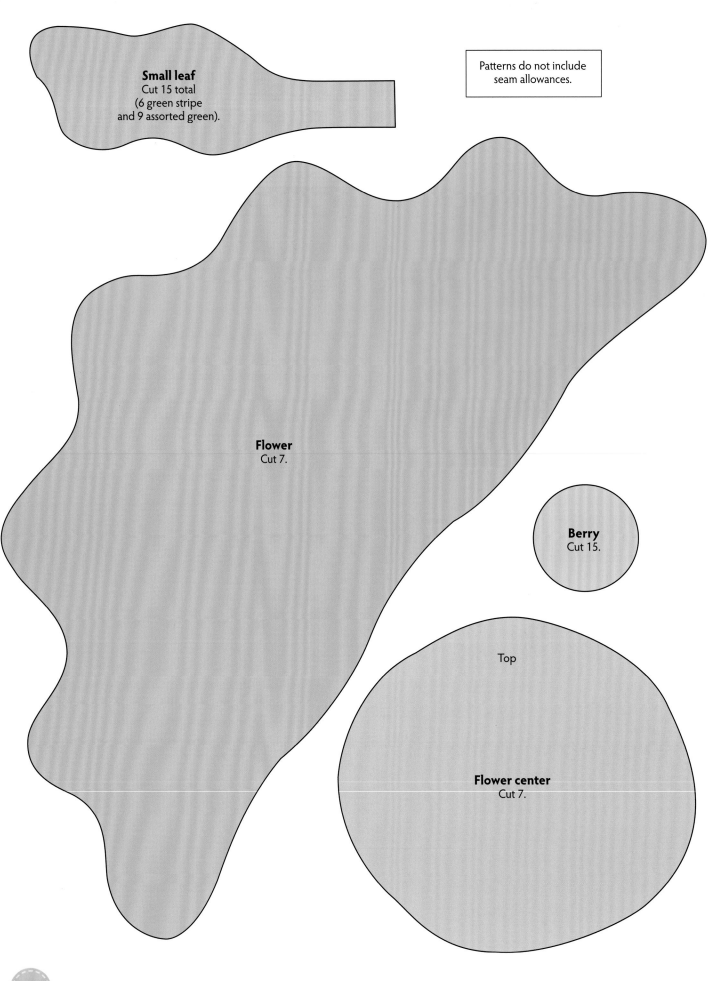

Small leaf
Cut 15 total
(6 green stripe
and 9 assorted green).

Patterns do not include
seam allowances.

Flower
Cut 7.

Berry
Cut 15.

Top

Flower center
Cut 7.

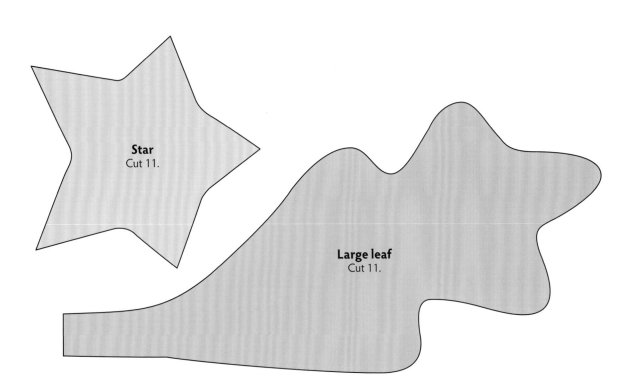

Star
Cut 11.

Large leaf
Cut 11.

Over, Under, Around, and Through

CHERYL WALL

Cheryl loves using lots of different fabrics in her quilts, but sometimes she challenges herself to limit the number of fabrics she can use in one design. For this quilt, she chose only four fabrics to produce a woven Churn Dash border around a checkered center.

Materials

Yardage is based on 42"-wide fabric.

2¼ yards of light fabric for blocks and outer border
1½ yards of medium fabric for blocks
1⅓ yards of dark fabric for blocks, inner border, and binding
⅓ yard of red fabric for blocks and corner squares
3¾ yards of backing fabric
62" × 62" piece of batting

One Dark or Two?

The same dark fabric was used for the blocks, inner border, and binding in this quilt. If you prefer to use a different fabric for the binding, you'll need 1 yard of dark fabric for the blocks and inner border and ½ yard of fabric for the binding.

Cutting

All measurements include ¼"-wide seam allowances.

From the light fabric, cut:
5 strips, 4½" × 42"
2 strips, 2½" × 42"
6 strips, 1½" × 42"
16 squares, 4½" × 4½"
32 squares, 3½" × 3½"
32 squares, 2½" × 2½"
16 rectangles, 1½" × 3½"

From the medium fabric, cut:
2 strips, 2½" × 42"
6 strips, 1½" × 42"
20 squares, 4½" × 4½"
32 squares, 3½" × 3½"
32 squares, 2½" × 2½"
16 rectangles, 1½" × 3½"

From the dark fabric, cut:
6 binding strips, 2¼" × 42"
7 strips, 1½" × 42"
2 strips, 4½" × 14"
4 strips, 1½" × 13"
50 rectangles, 1½" × 4½"

From the red fabric, cut:
4 squares, 4½" × 4½"
1 strip, 1½" × 14"
2 strips, 1½" × 13"
4 squares, 1½" × 1½"

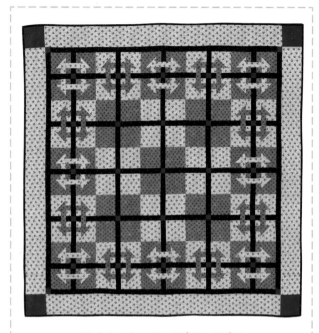

Finished quilt: 55½" × 55½"

Finished block: 9" × 9"

*Designed, pieced, and machine quilted
by Cheryl Wall*

Making the Blocks

This quilt includes four different block variations. The two different center blocks and the two different Churn Dash blocks are essentially the same, but color placement creates the checkered design and the woven border. After sewing each seam, press the seam allowances in the directions indicated by the arrows.

MAKING BLOCK 1

1 Place a 2½" light square on one corner of a 3½" medium square, right sides together. Sew diagonally from corner to corner as shown. Trim away the corner fabric, leaving a ¼" seam allowance. Make 32.

Make 32.

2 Sew two 1½" × 42" medium strips and one 1½" × 42" dark strip together lengthwise as shown to make a strip set. Crosscut the strip set into 16 segments, 2½" wide.

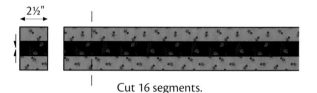

2½"

Cut 16 segments.

3 Sew a 1½" × 3½" light rectangle to each segment from step 2 as shown. Make 16.

Make 16.

4 Sew a unit from step 3 between two squares from step 1 as shown. Make 16 units.

   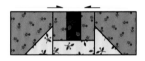

Make 16.

5 Sew one 2½" × 42" medium strip, one 1½" × 42" light strip, and one 1½" × 42" medium strip together lengthwise as shown to make a strip set. Make two of these strip sets. Crosscut the strip sets into 32 segments, 1½" wide.

1½"

Make 2 strip sets.
Cut 32 segments.

6 Sew a 1½" × 4½" dark rectangle between two segments from step 5 as shown. Make 16.

Make 16.

7 Sew two 1½" × 13" dark strips and one 1½" × 13" red strip together lengthwise as shown to make a strip set. Crosscut the strip set into eight segments, 1½" wide.

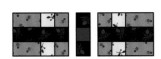

Cut 8 segments.

8 Sew one segment from step 7 between two units from step 6 to make a center unit. Make eight.

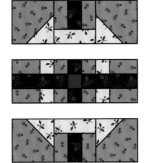

Make 8.

9 Sew a center unit between two units from step 4 to complete block 1, which should measure 9½" square, including seam allowances. Make a total of eight blocks.

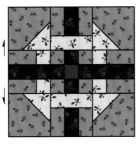

Block 1.
Make 8.

MAKING BLOCK 2

1 Referring to step 1 of "Making Block 1" on page 100, sew a 2½" medium square to one corner of a 3½" light square. Make 32.

2 Sew two 1½" × 42" light strips and one 1½" × 42" dark strip together lengthwise as shown to make a strip set. Crosscut the strip set into 16 segments, 2½" wide.

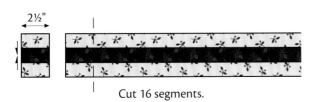

Cut 16 segments.

3 Sew a 1½" × 3½" medium rectangle to each segment from step 2. Make 16.

Make 16.

4 Sew a unit from step 3 between two squares from step 1 as shown. Make 16 units.

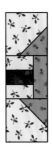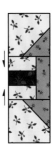

Make 16.

5 Sew one 2½" × 42" light strip, one 1½" × 42" medium strip, and one 1½" × 42" light strip together lengthwise as shown to make a strip set. Make two of these strip sets. Crosscut the strip sets into 32 segments, 1½" wide.

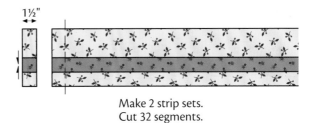

Make 2 strip sets.
Cut 32 segments.

6 Sew a 1½" × 4½" dark rectangle between two segments from step 5 as shown. Make 16.

Make 16.

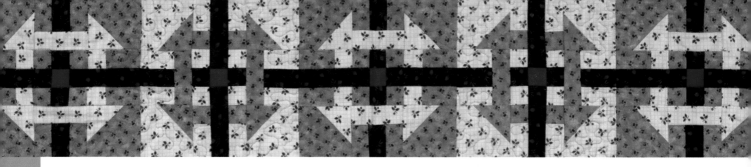

7 Sew two 1½" × 13" dark strips and one 1½" × 13" red strip together lengthwise as shown to make a strip set. Crosscut the strip set into eight segments, 1½" wide.

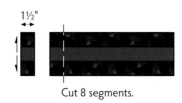

Cut 8 segments.

8 Sew one segment from step 7 between two units from step 6 to make a center unit. Make eight.

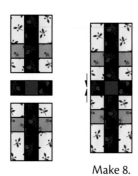

Make 8.

9 Sew a center unit between two units from step 4 to complete block 2, which should measure 9½" square, including seam allowances. Make a total of eight blocks.

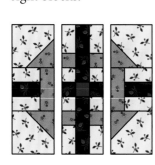
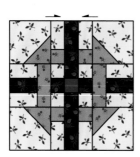

Block 2.
Make 8.

MAKING BLOCKS 3 AND 4

1 Sew two 4½" × 14" dark strips and one 1½" × 14" red strip together lengthwise as shown to make a strip set. Crosscut the strip set into nine segments, 1½" wide.

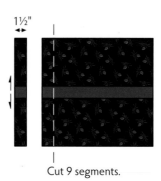

Cut 9 segments.

2 Sew a 1½" × 4½" dark rectangle between two 4½" medium squares. Make two. Sew one segment from step 1 between these two units to complete block 3, which should measure 9½" square, including seam allowances. Repeat to make a total of five blocks.

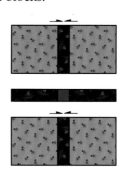
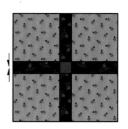

Block 3.
Make 5.

3 Sew a 1½" × 4½" dark rectangle between two 4½" light squares. Make two. Sew one segment from step 1 between these two units to complete block 4, which should measure 9½" square, including seam allowances. Repeat to make a total of four blocks.

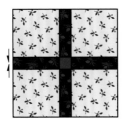

Block 4.
Make 4.

Assembling the Quilt Top

1 Lay out the blocks in five rows of five blocks each as shown in the quilt assembly diagram, alternating the light blocks and medium blocks and placing blocks 3 and 4 in the center.

2 Sew the blocks together in rows. Then sew the rows together. The quilt top should measure 45½" square, including seam allowances.

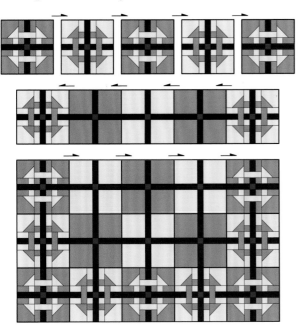

Quilt assembly

3 For the inner border, sew the remaining 1½"-wide dark strips together end to end. From the strip, cut four 45½"-long strips. Sew a strip to the top and bottom of the quilt top. Sew 1½" red squares to both ends of the two remaining dark strips. Sew these strips to the sides of the quilt top, pressing the seam allowances toward the border. The quilt top should measure 47½" square, including seam allowances.

4 For the outer border, sew the 4½"-wide light strips together end to end. From the strip, cut four 47½"-long strips. Sew a strip to the top and bottom of the quilt top. Sew 4½" red squares to both ends of the two remaining light strips and sew the strips to the sides of the quilt top. Press the seam allowances toward the border.

Finishing the Quilt

For detailed instructions on any of the finishing steps, go to ShopMartingale.com/HowtoQuilt for free information.

1 Layer the backing, batting, and quilt top; baste.

2 Quilt by hand or machine. The quilt shown is quilted with a stipple design.

3 Use the dark 2¼"-wide strips to make the binding; attach it to the quilt.

Finished quilt: 55" × 72"

Finished block: 6" × 6"

*By Kansas Troubles Quilters: designed by Lynne Hagmeier;
pieced by Lois Sprecker; machine quilted by Joy Johnson*

Triple Play

LYNNE HAGMEIER

Here's a chance to use precut 10" squares for Nine Patch blocks and block centers. The on-point blocks bring to mind a baseball diamond. The variation in scale and color placement among the blocks make for a unique and eye-catching quilt.

Materials

Yardage is based on 42"-wide fabric.

20 assorted medium-to-dark print 10" squares (navy, green, gold, purple, black, and pumpkin) for blocks
24 assorted tan-print 10" squares for blocks
22 assorted red-print 10" squares for blocks
⅔ yard of tan print for setting triangles
1¾ yards of black print for border and binding
3½ yards of fabric for backing
62" × 79" piece of batting

Cutting

All measurements include ¼"-wide seam allowances.

From the medium-to-dark print 10" squares, cut:
120 squares, 2½" × 2½"
60 squares, 1½" × 1½"
54 squares, 1" × 1"

From the assorted tan 10" squares, cut:
24 matching sets of 2 rectangles, 2" × 3½", and 2 rectangles, 2" × 6½"
264 squares, 1½" × 1½"
54 squares, 1" × 1"

From the assorted red 10" squares, cut:
15 matching sets of 2 rectangles, 2" × 3½", and 2 rectangles, 2" × 6½"
60 squares, 2½" × 2½"

From the tan print for setting triangles, cut:
5 squares, 9¾" × 9¾"; cut the squares into quarters diagonally to yield 20 triangles
2 squares, 5⅛" × 5⅛"; cut the squares in half diagonally to yield 4 triangles

From the black print, cut on the *lengthwise* grain:
4 strips, 6½" × 63"
5 strips, 2½" × 63"

Making the Framed 36 Patch Blocks

After sewing each seam, press seam allowances in the directions indicated by the arrows.

1 Lay out 18 assorted medium-to-dark and 18 tan 1" squares in six rows of six. Join the squares in each row. Join the rows. Make three.

Make 3.

2 Sew matching red 2" × 3½" rectangles to opposite sides of a 36-patch unit. Sew matching red 2" × 6½" rectangles to the top and bottom of the unit. Repeat to complete all three blocks, which should measure 6½" square, including seam allowances.

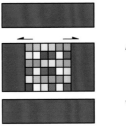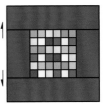

Make 3.

Assembling the Framed Nine Patch Blocks

1 Lay out five assorted medium-to-dark 1½" squares and four assorted tan 1½" squares in three rows of three, alternating the darks and lights. Join the squares in each row. Join the rows.

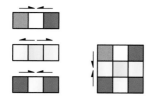

2 Sew matching red 2" × 3½" rectangles to opposite sides of the nine-patch unit. Sew matching red 2" × 6½" rectangles to the top and bottom of the unit. Make 12 red Framed Nine Patch blocks that measure 6½" square, including seam allowances.

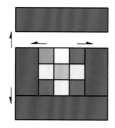

Make 12.

3 Repeat step 1 to assemble a nine-patch unit using nine assorted tan 1½" squares. Repeat step 2 to frame the unit with two matching tan 2" × 3½" rectangles and two matching tan 2" × 6½" rectangles. Make 24 tan Framed Nine Patch blocks that measure 6½" square, including seam allowances.

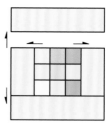

Make 24.

Making the Nine Patch Blocks

1 Lay out six assorted medium-to-dark 2½" squares and three assorted red 2½" squares in three rows of three squares each, placing the red squares diagonally across the block as shown. Sew the squares into rows. Sew the rows together to make a Nine Patch block. Make 16 blocks that measure 6½" square, including seam allowances.

Make 16.

2 Repeat step 1 to make four Nine Patch blocks with the red squares positioned in the center and two corners as shown.

Make 4.

Assembling the Quilt Top

1 Lay out the blocks on point as shown in the quilt assembly diagram, placing the Framed 36 Patch blocks in the center of the quilt, surrounded by tan Framed Nine Patch blocks, red Framed Nine Patch blocks, and Nine Patch blocks. Rotate the tan-framed blocks so that the seams don't butt up next to the seams in the red-framed blocks. Place the setting triangles along the edges and in the corners.

2 Join the blocks and side setting triangles in diagonal rows. Join the rows. Add the corner setting triangles.

3 Measure the quilt top vertically through the center. (It should measure 59⅞".) Trim two of the black 6½"-wide strips to that measurement. Sew the borders to the sides of the quilt; press the seam allowances toward the borders. Measure the quilt top horizontally through the center, including the borders just added. (It should measure 55".) Cut two strips to that measurement and sew the borders to the top and bottom of the quilt.

Finishing the Quilt

For detailed instructions on any of the finishing steps, go to ShopMartingale.com/HowtoQuilt for free information.

1 Layer the backing, batting, and quilt top; baste.

2 Quilt by hand or machine. The quilt shown is quilted in the ditch and has a variety of designs that highlight the shapes in the quilt, including a grid design in the blocks and a triangle design in the border.

3 Use the black 2½"-wide strips to make the binding; attach it to the quilt.

Quilt assembly

Peppermint Patties

VICKI BELLINO

This quilted confection features an assortment of mouthwatering fabrics in one easy-to-make block. The combination of brown, blue, and white prints brings to mind the combination of chocolate and mint—a classic candy favorite.

Materials

Yardage is based on 42"-wide fabric.

½ yard *each* of 6 assorted blue and brown prints
for blocks

1 yard of brown with blue polka-dot print for sashing
and binding

⅛ yard of diagonally striped fabric for sashing
squares

1¼ yards of blue-and-brown print for setting
triangles

3 yards of fabric for backing

50" × 64" piece of batting

Cutting

All measurements include ¼"-wide seam allowances.

**From *each* of the 6 assorted blue and brown
prints, cut:**

1 strip, 3½" × 42"; crosscut into:
   3 squares, 3½" × 3½" (18 total)
   6 rectangles, 1½" × 3½" (36 total)

1 strip, 1½" × 42"; crosscut into 6 rectangles,
   1½" × 5½" (36 total)

3 strips, 2½" × 42"; crosscut into:
   6 rectangles, 2½" × 5½" (36 total)
   6 rectangles, 2½" × 9½" (36 total)*

From the brown with blue polka-dot print, cut:

12 strips, 1½" × 42"; crosscut into 48 rectangles,
   1½" × 9½"

6 binding strips, 2" × 42"

From the diagonally striped fabric, cut:

2 strips, 1½" × 42"; crosscut into 31 squares, 1½" × 1½"

From the blue-and-brown print, cut:

2 strips, 15½" × 42"; crosscut into 3 squares,
   15½" × 15½"; cut the squares into quarters
   diagonally to make 12 side setting triangles
   (2 are extra)**

2 squares, 8¾" × 8¾"; cut the squares in half
   diagonally to yield 4 corner setting triangles**

*If you want to make 4 blocks with the same print
around the outer edges like this quilt, cut 8 rectangles
of each size from the chosen fabric. Cut just 4
rectangles of each size from one of the other fabrics.*

**The setting triangles are cut to the size needed; if you
want space beyond the block points, cut the squares
17" × 17" and 10½" × 10½".*

Making the Blocks

Make the blocks using the squares and rectangles from the assorted prints. Use a different print for each step. After sewing each seam, press seam allowances in the directions indicated by the arrows.

1 Sew 1½" × 3½" rectangles to the top and bottom of a contrasting 3½" square. Using the same print, sew a 1½" × 5½" rectangle to each side of the block.

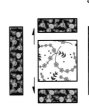

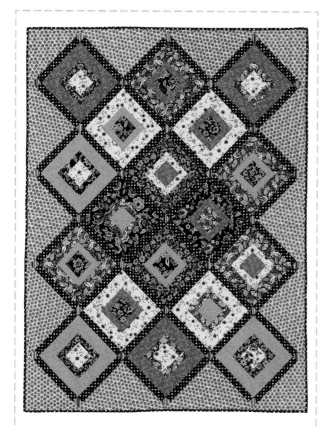

Finished quilt: 44" × 58"

Finished block: 9" × 9"

Quilted by Veronica Nurmi

3 Repeat steps 1 and 2 until all of the precut
squares and rectangles have been used to make
18 blocks.

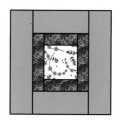

Make 18.

Assembling the Quilt Top

1 Arrange the blocks in diagonal rows, alternating
them with the polka-dot sashing rectangles and
striped sashing squares. Add the side and corner
setting triangles as shown in the quilt diagram.

2 Sew the blocks, sashing strips, sashing squares,
and setting triangles in diagonal rows. Sew the
rows together and add the corner triangles last.

2 Sew 2½" × 5½" rectangles in a contrasting color
to the top and bottom of the block, followed by
2½" × 9½" rectangles of the same print to each side.
The block should measure 9½" square, including
seam allowances.

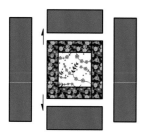 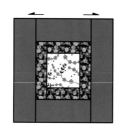

3 Trim and square up the quilt as needed. Be sure to leave at least ¼" beyond the block points. Leave about 1" if you cut your triangles oversized.

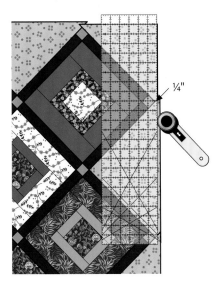

Finishing the Quilt

For detailed instructions on any of the finishing steps, go to ShopMartingale.com/HowtoQuilt for free information.

1 Layer the backing, batting, and quilt top; baste.

2 Quilt by hand or machine. The quilt shown is quilted with arcs in the blocks and a feathered arc pattern in the sashing.

3 Use the 2"-wide polka-dot strips to make the binding; attach it to the quilt.

Finished quilt: 71½" × 71½"
Finished block: 16" × 16"

Pieced by Nicole Reed;
machine quilted by Debbie Thornton

Decoy

CARRIE NELSON

Gather some 10" squares, add a background fabric, and you'll have all you need to assemble a lovely quilt top. A simple four-part recipe of lights, darks, mediums, and an accent color keeps fabric selection simple.

Materials

Yardage is based on 42"-wide fabric.

1½ yards of light background fabric for blocks
12 assorted accent 10" squares for star points and inner border
18 assorted dark 10" squares for star points
18 assorted light 10" squares for sashing
15 assorted medium 10" squares for outer border
¾ yard of fabric for binding
5 yards of fabric for backing
78" × 78" piece of batting

Cutting

All measurements include ¼"-wide seam allowances.

From the light background fabric, cut:
2 strips, 10" × 42"; crosscut into:
    5 squares, 10" × 10"
    2 lengthwise strips, 4½" × 30"; crosscut into
    8 squares, 4½" × 4½"
8 strips, 4½" × 42"; crosscut into 64 squares,
    4½" × 4½"

From *each* of 7 assorted accent squares, cut:
4 strips, 2" × 10" (28 total)
(Set the remaining 5 squares aside for half-square-triangle units.)

From *each* of the assorted dark squares, cut:
2 rectangles, 4½" × 8½" (36 total)

From *each* of the assorted light squares, cut:
3 rectangles, 3¼" × 10" (54 total; 2 are extra)

From *each* of the medium squares, cut:
2 rectangles, 5" × 10", from the *lengthwise* grain
    (30 total)

From the binding fabric, cut:
300" of 2"-wide bias binding

Making the Blocks

Use a scant ¼"-wide seam allowance throughout. After sewing each seam, press seam allowances in the directions indicated by the arrows.

1 Draw intersecting diagonal lines from corner to corner on the wrong side of a 10" background square. Layer the marked square with a 10" accent square, right sides together and edges aligned. Stitch a scant ¼" from each side of both lines. Carefully cut through the middle of the squares, both horizontally and vertically, as shown. Then cut the squares apart on the drawn lines to make eight half-square-triangle units. Trim the half-square-triangle units to 4½" square. (You'll have four matching units for this block and four units left over for another block.)

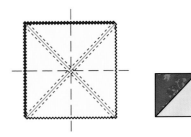

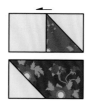

4 Sew together one background square and one half-square-triangle unit; then add a star-point unit as shown to complete a quadrant. Make four quadrants.

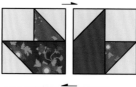

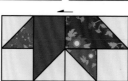

5 Join the quadrants into rows, and then sew the rows together to complete the block. The block should measure 16½" square. Repeat to make a total of nine blocks.

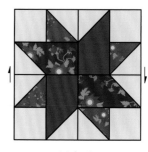

Make 9.

2 Draw a diagonal line from corner to corner on the wrong side of four 4½" background squares. Select two different pairs of matching dark rectangles. Place a marked square on one end of a dark rectangle as shown. Stitch along the marked line; trim, leaving a ¼" seam allowance. Make four star-point units, making sure the direction of the line is the same on all four units and that it matches the diagram.

Make 4.

Assembling the Quilt Center

1 To piece the sashing strips, divide the 3¼" × 10" light strips into two sets of 12 strips each and two sets of 14 strips each. Sew each set of strips together end to end to make a sashing strip. Press the seam allowances open. Make two strips about 110" long and two strips about 130" long.

2 From each 110"-long strip, cut six sashing strips, 3¼" × 16½", for a total of 12 sashing strips.

3 Join three blocks and four sashing strips from step 2 to make a block row as shown in the quilt assembly diagram on page 115. Make three of these rows.

3 Lay out the four star-point units, four half-square-triangle units, and four 4½" background squares as shown.

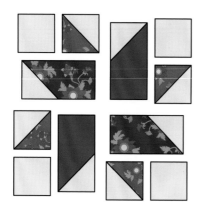

4 Measure the length of each block row; they should measure 59½". From the 130"-long sashing strips, cut four strips to that length.

5 Sew the block rows and sashing strips from step 4 together, alternating them as shown in the quilt assembly diagram. Press the seam allowances toward the sashing strips. The quilt top should measure 59½" square, including seam allowances.

Adding the Borders

1 For the inner border, sort the 2" × 10" accent strips into four sets of seven strips each. Sew each set of strips together end to end to make four long strips. Press the seam allowances open. For the side borders, trim two strips to measure 2" × 59½". For the top and bottom borders, trim two strips to measure 2" × 62½".

2 Sew the border strips to the sides, and then the top and bottom of the quilt top.

3 For the outer border, sort the 5" × 10" medium strips into the following groups:

- **Side borders:** two groups of seven strips each
- **Top and bottom borders:** two groups of eight strips each

Join each group of strips end to end to make four long strips. Press the seam allowances in one direction (or press them open). For the side borders,

trim the two shorter strips to measure 5" × 62½". For the top and bottom borders, trim the longer strips to measure 5" × 71½".

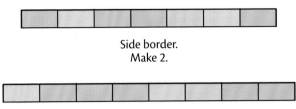

Side border.
Make 2.

Top/bottom border.
Make 2.

4 Sew the border strips to the sides, and then the top and bottom of the quilt top as shown in the quilt assembly diagram, keeping the pinked edges on the outside.

Finishing the Quilt

For detailed instructions on any of the finishing steps, go to ShopMartingale.com/HowtoQuilt for free information.

1 Layer the backing, batting, and quilt top; baste.

2 Quilt by hand or machine. The quilt shown is quilted with an allover pattern of swirls and spirals.

3 Use the 2"-wide binding strips to make the binding; attach it to the quilt.

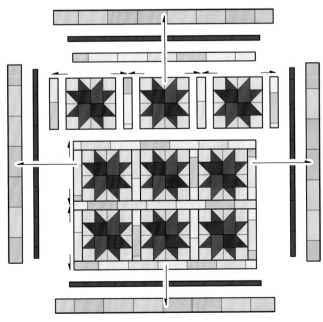

Quilt assembly

Prairie Picnic

NANCY MAHONEY

This cheerful quilt is sure to bring an extra ray of sunshine to your summer gatherings. Prairie flowers appliquéd in the center of patchwork blocks and fun prairie points come together to make this quilt a favorite addition at any picnic.

Materials

Yardage is based on 42"-wide fabric.

1¼ yards of cream-with-multicolored-dots print for blocks and middle border

⅝ yard of medium blue tone on tone for blocks and flower center appliqués

1⅛ yards of dark pink tone on tone for blocks, sashing, inner border, and border corner squares

⅜ yard of light blue tone on tone for blocks, sashing squares, and flower appliqués

¾ yard of light yellow checked fabric for block backgrounds

2 yards of dark red checked fabric for flower appliqués, prairie points, and binding

2 yards of multicolored floral for outer border*

⅜ yard of medium yellow tone on tone for flower appliqués

3⅝ yards of fabric for backing

60" × 77" piece of batting

34 red buttons, ½" diameter

1¾ yards of 16"-wide lightweight fusible web (optional)

Yardage amount is for one-piece lengthwise-cut border strips. If you don't mind seams in your outer border, 10⅛ yards is sufficient to cut crosswise strips.

Cutting

All measurements include ¼"-wide seam allowances. Cut all strips across the width of the fabric unless indicated otherwise.

From the cream-with-multicolored-dots print, cut:
3 strips, 6¾" × 42"; crosscut into 12 squares, 6¾" × 6¾". Cut the squares into quarters diagonally to yield 48 triangles.
5 strips, 3¼" × 42"

From the medium blue tone on tone, cut:
2 strips, 6¾" × 42"; crosscut into 6 squares, 6¾" × 6¾". Cut the squares into quarters diagonally to yield 24 triangles.

From the dark pink tone on tone, cut:
3 strips, 3⅝" × 42"; crosscut into 24 squares, 3⅝" × 3⅝". Cut the squares in half diagonally to yield 48 triangles.
3 strips, 2⅛" × 42"
6 strips, 1⅞" × 42"; crosscut 4 of the strips into 7 strips, 1⅞" × 17"
4 squares, 5½" × 5½"
4 squares, 3¼" × 3¼"

From the light blue tone on tone, cut:
2 strips, 3¼" × 42"; crosscut into 24 squares, 3¼" × 3¼"
2 squares, 1⅞" × 1⅞"

From the light yellow checked fabric, cut:
2 strips, 11½" × 42"; crosscut into 6 squares, 11½" × 11½"

From the dark red checked fabric, cut:
6 strips, 6" × 42"; crosscut into 34 squares, 6" × 6"
7 strips, 2" × 42"

From the *lengthwise* grain of the multicolored floral, cut:
2 strips, 5½" × 63"
2 strips, 5½" × 45" (or 6 strips, 5½" × 42", from the crosswise grain)

Finished quilt: 53⅝" × 71"
Finished block: 16½" × 16½"

Making the Blocks

After sewing each seam, press seam allowances in the directions indicated by the arrows.

1 Lay out two multicolored-dots triangles and one medium blue triangle as shown. Sew the triangles together, offsetting the points ¼" as shown. Make 24 units.

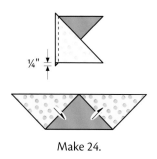

Make 24.

2 Sew dark pink triangles to the ends of each unit from step 1 as shown to complete the side units.

Make 24.

3 Lay out four side units, four light blue 3¼" squares, and one light yellow square as shown. Sew the pieces into rows. Join the rows. Make six blocks that are 17" square, including seam allowances.

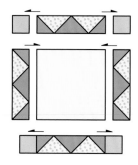
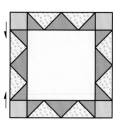

Make 6.

Adding the Appliqué

Use your preferred method of appliqué. Refer to the diagram for appliqué placement.

1 Using the patterns on page 121 and your preferred method, make 48 red petals, 8 light blue petals, 28 medium yellow buds, and 10 medium blue circles.

2 Fold each block in half vertically and horizontally to establish centering lines. Working in numerical order, appliqué the shapes in place on each block. Set aside the light blue petals and the remaining yellow buds and blue circles for the border.

Appliqué placement

Assembling the Quilt Top

1 Sew two blocks and one dark pink 17"-long sashing strip together as shown. Make three block rows.

Make 3.

2 Sew two dark pink 17"-long sashing strips and one light blue 1⅞" square together as shown. Make two sashing rows.

Make 2.

3 Refer to the quilt assembly diagram on page 120 to join the block rows and sashing rows.

4 Join the dark pink 2⅛"-wide strips end to end to make a long strip. Measure, cut, and sew inner-border strips to the sides of the quilt top. Using the dark pink 1⅞" × 42" strips, measure, cut, and sew inner-border strips to the top and bottom edges of the quilt top.

5 To make the prairie points, fold each dark red 6" square in half diagonally, wrong sides together. Fold the square diagonally again, forming a smaller triangle. Make 34 prairie points.

Fold. Fold.

Make 34.

6 Starting at one corner of the quilt, pin the cut edge of each prairie point to the cut edge of the quilt top, tucking the fold of one point into the opening of the next one. (They will overlap about ¼".) Make sure the folded edges of the triangles aim in the same direction as the first one and that the points are evenly spaced on each side. You should have 10 points on each side and seven points on the top and bottom of the quilt top. Using a walking foot and a scant ¼"-wide seam allowance, machine baste the prairie points to all four edges of the quilt top.

7 Measure the width of the quilt top and trim two of the multicolored-dots strips to that length. Join the three remaining multicolored-dots strips end to end to make a long strip. Measure the length of the quilt top and cut two strips to that length from the pieced strip. Sew the longer strips to the sides of the quilt top and press the seam allowances toward the inner border. Sew a dark pink 3¼" square to each end of the shorter strips. Sew the strips to the top and bottom edges of the quilt top. Press the seam allowances toward the inner border, with the prairie points pointing away from the quilt center.

9 Using the light blue petals, medium yellow buds, and medium blue circles you set aside earlier, appliqué the pieces in place as shown in the photo on page 118.

Finishing the Quilt

For detailed instructions on any of the finishing steps, go to ShopMartingale.com/HowtoQuilt for free information.

1 Layer the backing, batting, and quilt top; baste.

2 Quilt by hand or machine. The quilt shown features outline quilting around the appliqués, plus petals and arcs in the blocks and borders.

Quilting diagram

3 Use the dark red 2"-wide strips to make the binding; attach it to the quilt. Center a button on each prairie point, ¾" from the tip, and stitch it in place through the top and batting layers only.

8 Measure the length of the quilt top and trim the longer floral strips to that measurement for the side borders. Measure the width of the quilt top and trim the shorter floral strips to that measurement for the top and bottom borders. Sew the side borders to the quilt top. Add a dark pink 5½" square to each end of the shorter strips and sew them to the top and bottom edges of the quilt top for the outer border.

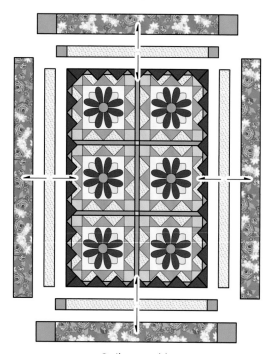

Quilt assembly

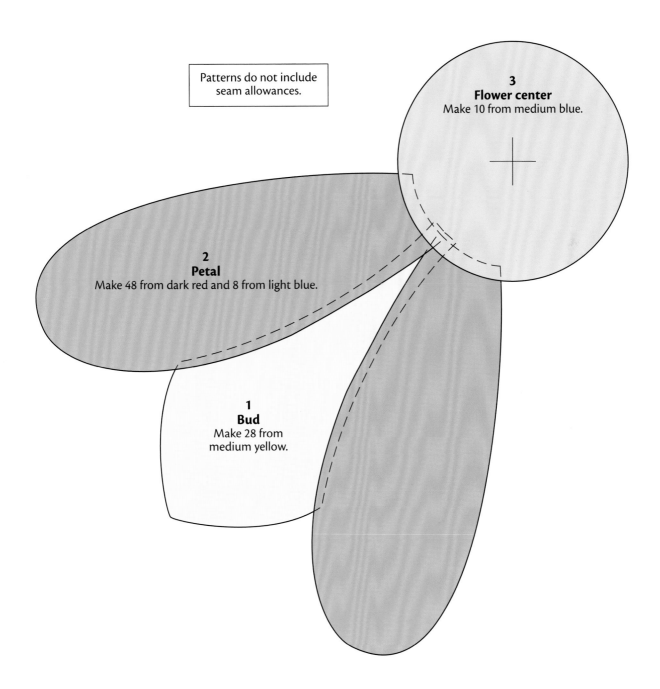

Patterns do not include seam allowances.

3
Flower center
Make 10 from medium blue.

2
Petal
Make 48 from dark red and 8 from light blue.

1
Bud
Make 28 from
medium yellow.

Finished quilt: 75½" × 75½"

Finished block: 9" × 9"

Pieced by Debbie Outlaw;
machine quilted by Maggie Honeyman

Lincoln

CARRIE NELSON

Mix a red, white, and blue color scheme, 13 stars, and little logs in Rail Fence blocks and you get a quilt called Lincoln. Stitch-and-flip triangles make the stars easy to stitch, and if you opt to use oh-so-convenient precut 10" squares, quiltmaking becomes even easier.

Materials

Yardage is based on 42"-wide fabric.

1½ yards of white print for Star block background and inner border

13 assorted-print 10" squares for star points

4 assorted-print 10" squares for star centers

64 assorted-print 10" squares for Rail Fence blocks and outer border

¾ yard of fabric for binding

5 yards of fabric for backing

84" × 84" piece of batting

Cutting

All measurements include ¼"-wide seam allowances.

From the white print for background and inner border, cut:

11 strips, 3⅛" × 42"; crosscut into:
    52 rectangles, 3⅛" × 4¼"
    52 squares, 3⅛" × 3⅛"

7 strips, 2" × 42"

From *each* of the 13 assorted-print squares for star points, cut:

3 strips, 3" × 10"; crosscut each strip into 3 squares, 3" × 3" (117 total; 13 are extra)

From *each* of the 4 assorted-print squares for star centers, cut:

2 strips, 4¼" × 10"; crosscut each strip into 2 squares, 4¼" × 4¼" (16 total; 3 are extra)

From *each* of 54 assorted-print squares for Rail Fence blocks and outer border, cut:

2 strips, 3½" × 10" (108 total)
1 strip, 2" × 10" (54 total)

From *each* of 9 assorted squares for Rail Fence blocks and outer border, cut:

4 strips, 2" × 10" (36 total; 2 are extra)

From the 1 remaining square for Rail Fence blocks and outer border, cut:

4 squares, 5" × 5"

From the binding fabric, cut:

315" of 2"-wide bias binding

Making the Star Blocks

Use a scant ¼"-wide seam allowance throughout. After sewing each seam, press seam allowances in the directions indicated by the arrows. For each block, you'll need the following pieces:

- **Background:** four 3⅛" × 4¼" rectangles and four 3⅛" squares
- **Star points:** eight matching 3" assorted-print squares
- **Star center:** one 4¼" assorted-print square

1. Draw a diagonal line from corner to corner on the wrong side of each 3" assorted-print square. Place a marked square on one end of a background rectangle as shown. Stitch along the marked line and trim, leaving a ¼" seam allowance.

Making the Rail Fence Blocks

Use a scant ¼"-wide seam allowance throughout.

1 Sort the 3½" × 10" strips into 36 groups of three strips each. Or you can randomly sew pairs of strips together. Just make sure you stop when you have 36 pairs of strips.

2 Join three strips as shown to make a Rail Fence block. Trim the block to measure 9½" square. Repeat to make a total of 36 blocks.

Make 36.

2 In the same manner, sew a marked square to the other end of the rectangle as shown to make a star-point unit. The seam allowance where the two triangles overlap will be wider than ¼". Make four matching star-point units for each block (52 total).

Make 52.

3 Lay out four matching star points, four background squares, and one 4¼" square as shown. Join the pieces into rows, and then sew the rows together to complete a Star block. The block should measure 9½" square, including seam allowances. Repeat to make a total of 13 blocks.

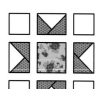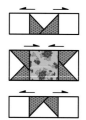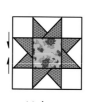

Make 13.

Assembling the Quilt Top

1 Lay out the Rail Fence and Star blocks in seven rows of seven blocks each, alternating them as shown and rotating the Rail Fence blocks as needed. Sew the blocks together in rows. Make the number of rows indicated for each combination of blocks. Note that the seams on the Rail Fence blocks and the Star blocks are not intended to line up.

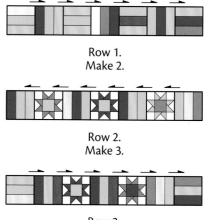

Row 1.
Make 2.

Row 2.
Make 3.

Row 3.
Make 2.

2 Sew the rows together. The quilt top should measure 63½" square, including seam allowances.

Adding the Borders

1 For the inner border, sew the 2"-wide white strips together end to end. From the long strip, cut two strips, 63½" long, and sew them to the sides of the quilt top. Cut two 66½" strips and sew them to the top and bottom of the quilt top. The quilt top should measure 66½" square, including seam allowances.

2 For the outer border, sort the 2" × 10" assorted strips to make two sets of 44 strips each. Select one set of strips and sort it into four groups of 11 strips each. Join each group of 11 strips side by side as shown. Make four pieced sections. Each section should measure 10" × 17". Repeat to make a second set of four pieced sections.

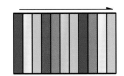

Make 8.

3 Cut each pieced section in half lengthwise as shown to make 16 pieced outer-border strips, and then sort them into two groups of two matching sets.

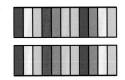

4 Join one set of strips to make a 5" × 66½" pieced outer-border strip (if you started with precut squares, keep the pinked edges on the same side). Repeat to make a total of four outer-border strips.

5 Sew two outer-border strips to the sides of the quilt top, keeping the pinked edges on the outside.

6 Join 5" squares to the ends of the two remaining outer-border strips. Sew these borders to the top and bottom of the quilt top.

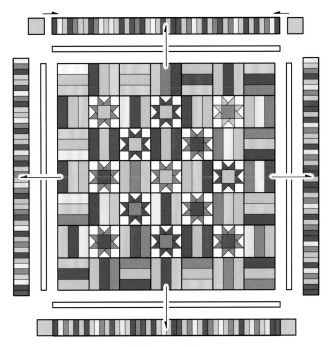

Quilt assembly

Finishing the Quilt

For detailed instructions on any of the finishing steps, go to ShopMartingale.com/HowtoQuilt for free information.

1 Layer the backing, batting, and quilt top; baste.

2 Quilt by hand or machine. The quilt shown is quilted with an allover pattern of curves and loops.

3 Use the 2"-wide strips to make the binding; attach it to the quilt.

Finished quilt: 65½" × 65½"

Finished block: 10" × 10"

Designed and pieced by Krystal Stahl;
quilted by Diane Selman of MyLongArm.com

Hazelwood Stars

KRYSTAL STAHL

Rotating these striking blocks throughout the quilt will create a secondary pattern of interlocking white chevrons, adding movement to the design. For a super scrappy effect, use a fat quarter in a different print for each block.

Materials

Yardage is based on 42"-wide fabric. Fat quarters are 18" × 21" and fat eighths are 9" × 21".

36 fat eighths *OR* fat quarters of assorted bright prints for blocks*
4⅝ yards of white tone on tone for blocks and border
⅝ yard of aqua dot for binding
4⅛ yards of fabric for backing
72" × 72" piece of batting

Fat eighths are sufficient if you cut carefully.

Cutting

All measurements include ¼"-wide seam allowances. Group the matching pieces from each fat eighth together; one block is made from each print.

From *each* of the 36 bright prints, refer to the diagram at right to cut:
2 squares, 3⅜" × 3⅜" (72 total)
2 rectangles, 3" × 5½" (72 total)
8 squares, 3" × 3" (288 total)

From the *lengthwise* grain of the white tone on tone, cut:
2 strips, 3" × 65½"
2 strips, 3" × 60½"
4 strips, 3⅜" × 65"; crosscut into 72 squares, 3⅜" × 3⅜"
2 strips, 5½" × 65"; crosscut into 22 squares, 5½" × 5½"

From the remainder of the white tone on tone, cut:
2 strips, 5½" × 42"; crosscut into 14 squares, 5½" × 5½"
23 strips, 3" × 42"; crosscut into:
   72 rectangles, 3" × 5½"
   144 squares, 3" × 3"

From the aqua dot, cut:
8 strips, 2½" × 42"

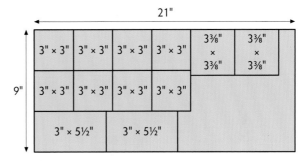

Cutting from a fat eighth

Making the Blocks

Use matching print pieces for each block. After sewing each seam, press seam allowances in the directions indicated by the arrows.

1 Draw a diagonal line from corner to corner on the wrong side of four matching print 3" squares. Place the marked squares on opposite corners of a white 5½" square with right sides together as shown. Sew on the marked lines. Trim ¼" from each seam. Sew the remaining marked squares to the remaining corners in the same manner. The block center should measure 5½" square, including seam allowances.

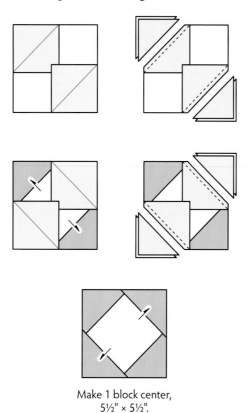

Make 1 block center,
5½" × 5½".

2 Draw a diagonal line from corner to corner on the wrong side of a white 3⅜" square. Layer the marked square right sides together with a print 3⅜" square. Sew ¼" from each side of the marked line. Cut the squares apart on the marked line to yield two half-square-triangle units. Trim the units to measure 3" square. Repeat to make four units.

Make 4 units.

3 Draw a diagonal line from corner to corner on the wrong side of four matching print 3" squares. Place a marked square right sides together on one end of a white 3" × 5½" rectangle as shown. Stitch on the marked line. Trim ¼" from the seam. Repeat to add a matching print square to the opposite end of the rectangle. The flying-geese unit should measure 3" × 5½". Make two. In the same manner, make two flying-geese units using white 3" squares and print 3" × 5½" rectangles.

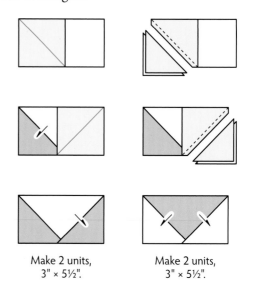

Make 2 units,
3" × 5½".

Make 2 units,
3" × 5½".

4 Lay out the four half-square-triangle units, the four flying-geese units, and the block center in three rows as shown. Join the units into rows, and then join the rows. The block should measure 10½" square, including seam allowances. Repeat with each set of matching print pieces to make 36 blocks.

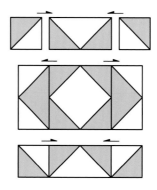 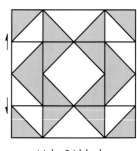

Make 36 blocks,
10½" × 10½".

Assembling the Quilt Top

1 Lay out the blocks in six rows of six, rotating alternate blocks a quarter turn as shown in the quilt assembly diagram. Join the blocks in each row, and then join the rows. The quilt center should measure 60½" square, including seam allowances.

2 Sew the white 60½"-long strips to the sides of the quilt center, and then add the white 65½"-long strips to the top and bottom. The finished quilt top should measure 65½" square.

Finishing the Quilt

For detailed instructions on any of the finishing steps, go to ShopMartingale.com/HowtoQuilt for free information.

1 Layer the backing, batting, and quilt top; baste.

2 Quilt by hand or machine. The quilt shown is quilted with an allover swirl design.

3 Use the aqua 2½"-wide strips to make the binding; attach it to the quilt.

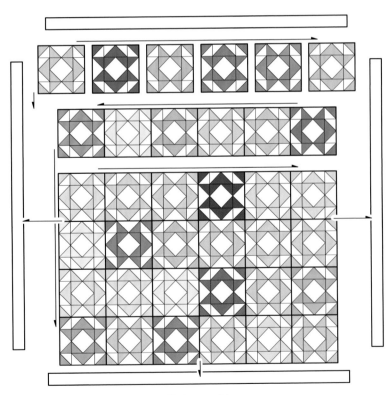

Quilt assembly

Finished quilt: 64½" × 64½"

Finished block: 8" × 8"

Made with the Handmade fabric line by Bonnie and Camille

Cakewalk

MARY JACOBSON AND BARBARA GROVES
OF ME AND MY SISTER DESIGNS

Here you have it—think of the block centers as the squares in the path of a cakewalk. Buy a ticket, step on a square, and walk until the music stops. Whoever is standing on the winning square wins the cake!

Materials

Yardage is based on 42"-wide fabric.

1¼ yards of white solid for blocks and inner border
36 squares, 10" × 10", of assorted prints for blocks*
2 yards of turquoise print for outer border**
⅝ yard of red print for binding
4⅛ yards of fabric for backing
71" × 71" piece of batting

A Moda Layer Cake contains 42 squares, 10" × 10".

**The outer-border fabric shown was cut on the lengthwise grain. If you wish to cut the borders crosswise and piece strips together, you'll need just 1¼ yards.*

Cutting

All measurements include ¼"-wide seam allowances.

From the white solid, cut:
9 strips, 2½" × 42"; crosscut into 144 squares, 2½" × 2½"
6 strips, 2½" × 42"

From *each* of the print 10" squares, cut:
4 squares, 4½" × 4½" (144 total)*

From the turquoise print, cut:
6 strips, 6½" × 42"

From the red print, cut:
7 strips, 2¼" × 42"

Keep like prints together.

Making the Blocks

Use a small stitch length throughout. After sewing each seam, press seam allowances in the directions indicated by the arrows.

1 Draw a diagonal line on the wrong side of each white 2½" square. With right sides together, place a marked square on one corner of each print 4½" square as shown. Stitch on the marked line. Trim the seam allowance to ¼", flip, and press. Make 144 units.

Make 144 units.

2 Arrange and sew four matching units together as shown. The block should measure 8½" square, including seam allowances. Make a total of 36 blocks.

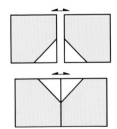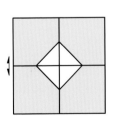

Make 36 blocks,
8½" x 8½".

Assembling the Quilt Center

1 Referring to the quilt assembly diagram below, arrange the blocks in six rows of six blocks each. Sew the blocks in each row together.

2 Sew the rows together. The quilt top should now measure 48½" square.

Adding the Borders

1 For the inner border, piece the six white 2½" × 42" strips together end to end. From this length, cut two strips, 48½" long, and sew them to the sides of the quilt top.

2 From the remainder of the white strip, cut two strips, 52½" long, and sew them to the top and bottom of the quilt top. The quilt top should now measure 52½" square, including seam allowances.

3 For the outer border, piece the six turquoise 6½" × 42" strips together end to end. From this length, cut two strips, 52½" long, and sew them to the sides of the quilt top.

4 From the remainder of the turquoise strip, cut two strips, 64½" long, and sew them to the top and bottom of the quilt top. The completed quilt top should measure 64½" square.

Finishing the Quilt

For detailed instructions on any of the finishing steps, go to ShopMartingale.com/HowtoQuilt for free information.

1 Layer the backing, batting, and quilt top; baste.

2 Quilt by hand or machine. The quilt shown is quilted with four hearts in the white squares surrounded by feathered wreath designs. The inner border is quilted with hearts and the outer border features a feathered vine.

3 Use the red 2¼"-wide strips to make the binding; attach it to the quilt.

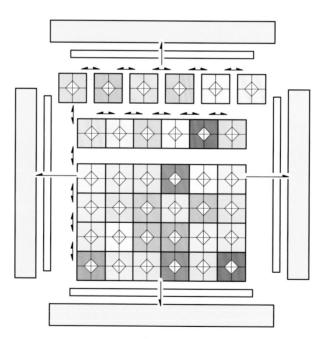

Quilt assembly

Bespoke

COREY YODER

Enjoy using a combination of half-square-triangle units and four-patch units to create two Nine Patch block variations. The block combination makes this charming quilt much easier to piece than it looks!

Materials

Yardage is based on 42"-wide fabric.

3 yards of white solid for blocks
¼ yard *each* of 12 assorted bright prints
    for Star blocks
1 yard of gray polka dot for Chain blocks
⅝ yard of aqua-and-white stripe for binding
3⅞ yards of fabric for backing
68" × 80" piece of batting

Cutting

All measurements include ¼"-wide seam allowances.

From the white solid, cut:
8 strips, 5" × 42"; crosscut into 60 squares, 5" × 5"
8 strips, 4½" × 42"; crosscut into 60 squares,
    4½" × 4½"
8 strips, 2½" × 42"

From *each* of the assorted bright prints, cut:
1 strip, 5" × 42"; crosscut into:
    5 squares, 5" × 5" (60 total)
    1 square, 4½" × 4½" (12 total)

From the remainder of the bright-print strips, cut a total of:
    3 squares, 4½" × 4½"

From the gray polka dot, cut:
2 strips, 4½" × 42"; crosscut into 15 squares,
    4½" × 4½"
8 strips, 2½" × 42"

From the aqua-and-white stripe, cut:
7 strips, 2½" × 42"

Making the Star Blocks

After sewing each seam, press seam allowances in the directions indicated by the arrows.

1 Draw a diagonal line from corner to corner on the wrong side of each white 5" square.

2 With right sides together, place a marked white square on top of a print 5" square. Sew ¼" from each side of the drawn line. Cut along the drawn line to yield two half-square-triangle units. Trim the units to 4½" square. Make 120 units.

Make 120.

3 Lay out eight assorted half-square-triangle units and one print 4½" square in three rows as shown. Join the units in each row. Join the rows. Make 15 blocks, which should measure 12½" square, including seam allowances.

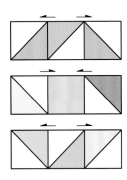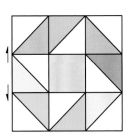

Make 15.

Finished quilt: 60½" × 72½"

Finished block: 12" × 12"

Designed by Corey Yoder; quilted by Abby Latimer

Making the Chain Blocks

1 Join one gray 2½" × 42" strip and one white 2½" × 42" strip to create a strip set. Make eight strip sets. Crosscut the strip sets into 120 segments, 2½" wide.

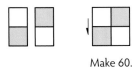

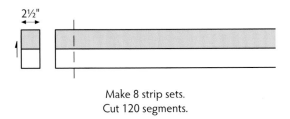

Make 8 strip sets.
Cut 120 segments.

2 Join two segments as shown to make a four-patch unit measuring 4½" square, including seam allowances. Make 60 units.

Make 60.

3 Lay out four of the four-patch units, four white 4½" squares, and one gray 4½" square. Join the units in each row. Join the rows. Make 15 blocks, which should measure 12½" square, including seam allowances.

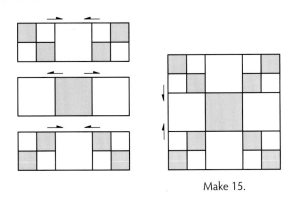

Make 15.

Assembling the Quilt Top

Arrange the blocks in six rows of five blocks each, alternating the blocks as shown in the quilt assembly diagram. Join the blocks in each row. Join the rows.

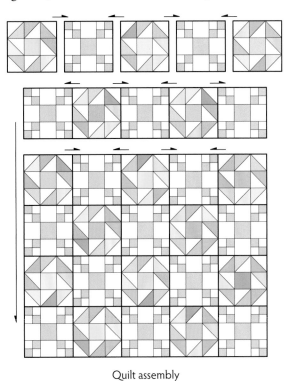

Quilt assembly

Finishing the Quilt

For detailed instructions on any of the finishing steps, go to ShopMartingale.com/HowtoQuilt for free information.

1 Layer the backing, batting, and quilt top; baste.

2 Quilt by hand or machine. The quilt shown is quilted with overall spiral design.

3 Use the aqua-and-white 2½"-wide strips to make the binding; attach it to the quilt.

Precious Peonies

NANCY MAHONEY

Pretty floral fabrics, graceful appliqué, and simple pieced blocks combine to make this sweet quilt the perfect choice for any decor. Use it as a wall hanging to brighten a room, or snuggle under it and dream of summer on a cold winter day.

Materials

Yardage is based on 42"-wide fabric.

1⅛ yards of pink floral for blocks and sashing squares

1⅔ yards of cream print for blocks and middle border

½ yard of pink tone on tone for blocks

½ yard of green fabric A for blocks

⅞ yard of light green floral for sashing and inner border

2¼ yards of dark green floral for outer border and binding

½ yard of green fabric B for leaf appliqués

½ yard of medium pink fabric for flower appliqués

¼ yard of dark pink fabric for flower appliqués

4½ yards of fabric for backing

75" × 75" piece of batting

2 yards of 16"-wide lightweight fusible web (optional)

Cutting

All measurements include ¼"-wide seam allowances. Cut all strips across the width of the fabric unless indicated otherwise.

From the pink floral, cut:

3 strips, 8¼" × 42"; crosscut into:
   9 squares, 8¼" × 8¼"
   4 squares, 2" × 2"
3 strips, 3¼" × 42"; crosscut into 36 squares, 3¼" × 3¼"

From the pink tone on tone, cut:

4 strips, 3⅝" × 42"; crosscut into 36 squares, 3⅝" × 3⅝". Cut the squares in half diagonally to yield 72 half-square triangles.

From the cream print, cut:

3 strips, 6⅜" × 42"; crosscut into 18 squares, 6⅜" × 6⅜". Cut the squares in half diagonally to yield 36 half-square triangles.
7 strips, 3⅝" × 42"; crosscut into 72 squares, 3⅝" × 3⅝". Cut the squares in half diagonally to yield 144 half-square triangles.
6 strips, 1½" × 42"

From green fabric A, cut:

2 strips, 6¾" × 42"; crosscut into 9 squares, 6¾" × 6¾". Cut the squares into quarters diagonally to yield 36 triangles.

From the light green floral, cut:

12 strips, 2" × 42"; crosscut 6 of the strips into 12 strips, 2" × 17"

From the *lengthwise* grain of the dark green floral, cut:

2 strips, 5¾" × 72"
2 strips, 5¾" × 61"
5 strips, 2" × 58"

Making the Blocks

After sewing each seam, press seam allowances in the directions indicated by the arrows.

1 Fold each pink floral 8¼" square in half vertically and horizontally and finger-press the folds to establish centering lines. Fold each cream 6⅜" triangle in half and finger-press the fold to mark the center on the long side. Sew cream triangles to opposite sides of a pink floral square, aligning the creased lines. Sew cream triangles to the remaining

Finished quilt: 68½" × 68½"

Finished block: 16½" × 16½"

*Pieced and appliquéd by Nancy Mahoney;
machine quilted by Nan Moore*

sides of the square to complete a center unit. The unit should measure 11½" square, including seam allowances. Make nine center units.

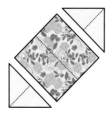 

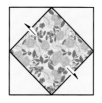

Make 9.

2 Join a cream 3⅝" triangle to a pink tone-on-tone triangle to make a half-square-triangle unit. The unit should measure 3¼" square, including seam allowances. Make 72 units.

Make 72.

3 Sew cream 3⅝" triangles to the short sides of a green fabric A triangle to make a flying-geese unit. The unit should measure 3¼" × 6", including seam allowances. Make 36 units.

Make 36.

4 Join two half-square triangles and one flying-geese unit as shown to make a side unit. Make 36 units.

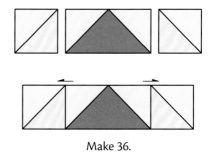

Make 36.

5 Lay out four pink floral 3¼" squares, four side units from step 4, and one center unit from step 1 as shown. Sew the pieces together into rows, and then sew the rows together to complete the block, which should measure 17" square, including seam allowances. Make nine blocks.

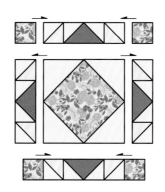 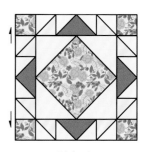

Make 9.

Adding the Appliqué

Use your preferred method of appliqué. Refer to the diagram below for appliqué placement.

1 Using the patterns on page 140 and your preferred method, make 36 green B leaves, 36 medium pink outer petals, and 36 dark pink center petals.

2 Appliqué the shapes in place on each block, working in numerical order.

Appliqué placement

Assembling the Quilt Top

1 Sew three blocks and two light green floral 2" × 17" sashing strips together, alternating them as shown. Make three block rows.

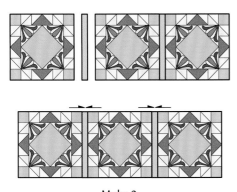

Make 3.

2 Sew three light green 2" × 17" sashing strips and two pink floral 2" squares together, alternating them as shown. Make two sashing rows.

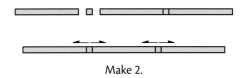

Make 2.

3 Refer to the quilt assembly diagram to join the block rows and sashing rows. The quilt top should measure 53" square, including seam allowances.

4 Join the remaining light green 2"-wide strips end to end to make a long strip. Measure, cut, and sew the strips for the inner border, attaching them to the sides and then to the top and bottom edges of the quilt top.

5 Join the cream 1½"-wide strips end to end to make a long strip. Measure, cut, and sew strips for the middle border, attaching them to the sides, and then to the top and bottom edges of the quilt top.

6 Using the dark green 5¾"-wide strips, measure and cut the shorter strips and sew them to the sides of the quilt top. Repeat to add the longer strips to the top and bottom edges of the quilt top to complete the outer border.

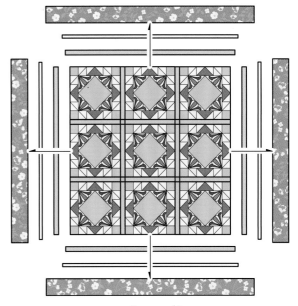

Quilt assembly

Finishing the Quilt

For detailed instructions on any of the finishing steps, go to ShopMartingale.com/HowtoQuilt for free information.

1 Layer the backing, batting, and quilt top; baste.

2 Quilt by hand or machine. The quilt shown is quilted with loops and scallops. See the quilting suggestion at right.

3 Use the dark green 2"-wide strips to make the binding; attach it to the quilt.

Quilting diagram

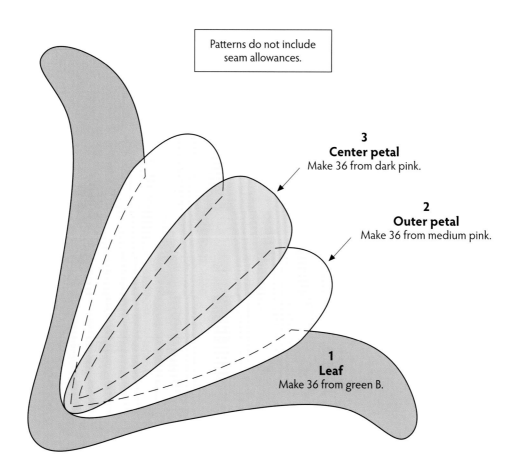

Patterns do not include seam allowances.

3
Center petal
Make 36 from dark pink.

2
Outer petal
Make 36 from medium pink.

1
Leaf
Make 36 from green B.

Four Generations

AMANDA NIEDERHAUSER

The quiltmaker designed this quilt as a celebration of the four generations of women in her family who all share a love of sewing, represented by the cute clusters of four houses in each block. She took inspiration for the Irish Chain blocks from a treasured quilt she inherited from her great grandmother.

Cutting

All measurements include ¼"-wide seam allowances.

From the white solid, cut:
2 strips, 6½" × 42"
18 strips, 2½" × 42"; crosscut *14* of the strips into:
    30 rectangles, 2½" × 6½"
    120 squares, 2½" × 2½"
10 strips, 1½" × 42"; crosscut into 30 strips,
    1½" × 10½"

From 9 of the bright prints, cut:
1 strip, 2½" × 42" (9 total)

From *each* of the 15 bright prints, cut:
4 rectangles, 2½" × 4½" (60 total)
8 rectangles, 2" × 3½" (120 total)
4 rectangles, 1½" × 2½" (60 total)
4 squares, 1½" × 1½" (60 total)

From the blue print, cut:
6 strips, 2½" × 42"

Materials

Yardage is based on 42"-wide fabric.

2¼ yards of white solid for background
¼ yard *each* of 15 bright prints for blocks*
⅝ yard of blue print for binding
3⅜ yards of fabric for backing
56" × 66" piece of batting

For a scrappier effect, incorporate more prints.

Finished quilt: 50½" × 60½"

Finished blocks: 10" × 10"

The Big Book of Lap Quilts

Making the Irish Chain Blocks

After sewing each seam, press seam allowances in the directions indicated by the arrows.

1 Sew a white 2½" × 42" strip between two different bright 2½" × 42" strips. The strip set should measure 6½" × 42". Make two. From the strip sets, crosscut a total of 30 A segments, 2½" wide.

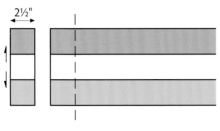

Make 2 strip sets.
Cut 30 A segments, 2½" × 6½".

2 Sew a bright 2½" × 42" strip between two white 2½" × 42" strips. The strip set should measure 6½" × 42". From the strip set, crosscut 15 B segments, 2½" wide.

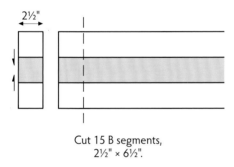

Cut 15 B segments,
2½" × 6½".

3 Sew a B segment between two A segments to make a nine-patch unit. Repeat to make 15 nine-patch units that measure 6½" square, including seam allowances.

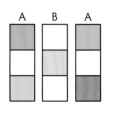

Make 15 units,
6½" × 6½".

4 Sew white 2½" × 6½" rectangles to the top and bottom of a nine-patch unit. The unit should measure 6½" × 10½", including seam allowances. Make 15.

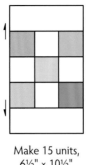

Make 15 units,
6½" × 10½".

5 Sew a white 6½" × 42" strip between two different bright 2½" × 42" strips. The strip set should measure 10½" × 42". Make two. From the strip sets, crosscut a total of 30 segments, 2½" wide.

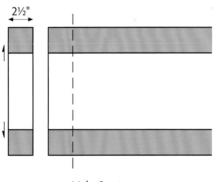

Make 2 strip sets.
Cut 30 segments, 2½" × 10½".

6 Sew one segment from each step 5 strip set to each long side of a unit from step 4. Repeat to make 15 blocks that measure 10½" square, including seam allowances.

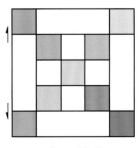

Make 15 blocks,
10½" × 10½".

Making the House Blocks

1 Draw a diagonal line from corner to corner on the wrong side of the white 2½" squares. Place a marked square on one end of a bright 2½" × 4½" rectangle, orienting the drawn line as shown. Sew along the drawn line. Trim the seam allowances to ¼", and then press.

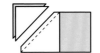

Make 60 units,
2½" × 4½".

2 Place a second square on the opposite end of the rectangle, orienting the line as shown. Sew, trim, and press. The unit should measure 2½" × 4½", including seam allowances. Make 60 flying-geese units.

Make 60 units,
2½" × 4½".

3 Select a matching set of two bright 2" × 3½" rectangles and one 1½" square. Select a contrasting bright 1½" × 2½" rectangle. Sew the 1½" square to the top of the 1½" × 2½" rectangle. The unit should measure 1½" × 3½". Sew the print 2" × 3½" rectangles to the sides of the pieced unit. The house unit should measure 3½" × 4½", including seam allowances. Make 60 units.

Make 60 units,
3½" × 4½".

4 Sew a contrasting flying-geese unit to the top of each house unit. The house unit should now measure 4½" × 5½", including the seam allowances. Make 60. For easier seam matching in step 5, press the seam allowances on half of the units toward the roofs, and on the other half toward the houses.

Make 60 units,
4½" × 5½".

5 Lay out two rows of two house units. Join the units in each row, and then join the rows. The four-house unit should measure 8½" × 10½", including seam allowances.

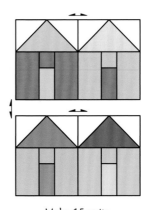

Make 15 units,
8½" × 10½".

6 Sew white 1½" × 10½" strips to the left and right sides of the four-house unit. The block should measure 10½" square, including seam allowances. Make 15 House blocks.

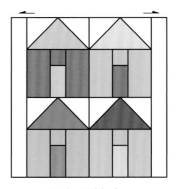

Make 15 blocks,
10½" × 10½".

Assembling the Quilt Top

Lay out the blocks in six rows of five, alternating the Irish Chain and House blocks as shown in the quilt assembly diagram. Join the blocks in each row, and then join the rows. The quilt top should measure 50½" × 60½".

Finishing the Quilt

For detailed instructions on any of the finishing steps, go to ShopMartingale.com/HowtoQuilt for free information.

1 Layer the backing, batting, and quilt top; baste.

2 Quilt by hand or machine. The quilt shown is quilted with an allover swirl and paisley design.

3 Use the blue 2½"-wide strips to make the binding; attach it to the quilt.

Quilt assembly

Finished quilt: 56½" × 56½"
Finished block: 16" × 16"

Made with the Grow fabric line by Me and My Sister Designs

Squared Circles

MARY JACOBSON AND BARBARA GROVES
OF ME AND MY SISTER DESIGNS

When cutting a cake, some folks like to cut off the corners first. Why, you ask? It's because the corners have the most frosting! Corners are crucial to this quilt as well. You'll make the blocks simply by sewing squares to the corners and cutting them off. Grab a big glass of milk and have some quality time cutting and sewing this "cakey" sweet quilt.

Materials

Yardage is based on 42"-wide fabric.

36 squares, 10" × 10", of assorted prints for blocks*

1⅔ yards of white solid for blocks, sashing, and border

¼ yard of orange print for block centers and sashing squares

½ yard of turquoise print for binding

3⅝ yards of fabric for backing

63" × 63" piece of batting

A Moda Layer Cake contains 42 squares, 10" × 10".

Cutting

All measurements include ¼"-wide seam allowances.

From *each* of the print 10" squares, cut:

2 triangles* (72 total)

From the white solid, cut:

7 strips, 3½" × 42"; crosscut into 72 squares, 3½" × 3½"

12 strips, 2½" × 42"; crosscut 6 strips into 12 strips, 2½" × 16½"

From the orange print, cut:

3 strips, 2½" × 42"; crosscut into 40 squares, 2½" × 2½"

From the turquoise print, cut:

6 strips, 2¼" × 42"

Cut each square in half diagonally.

Making the Blocks

After sewing each seam, press seam allowances in the directions indicated by the arrows. For each block, select the following:

- 8 print triangles
- 8 white 3½" squares
- 4 orange 2½" squares

1 With right sides together, sew two triangles together to make a half-square-triangle unit. Make four and trim the units to 8½" square.

Make 4 units, 8½" x 8½".

2 Draw a diagonal line from corner to corner on the wrong side of eight white 3½" squares. Place marked white squares right sides together on opposite corners of each half-square-triangle unit. Stitch on the marked lines. Trim seam allowances to ¼" and press. Make four.

Make 4.

147

3 Draw a diagonal line from corner to corner on the wrong side of four orange 2½" squares. Repeat step 3 to sew a marked square on one white corner of each unit. Make four.

Make 4.

4 Arrange and sew the four units into a block as shown. The block should measure 16½" square, including seam allowances. Make a total of nine blocks.

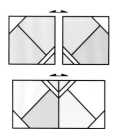

Make 9 blocks,
16½" x 16½".

Assembling the Quilt Top

1 Arrange and sew three blocks and two white 2½" × 16" sashing strips into a row. Make three rows that measure 16½" × 52½", including seam allowances.

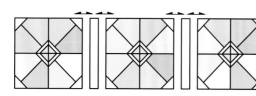

Make 3 rows,
16½" x 52½".

2 Sew three white 2½" × 16½" strips and two orange 2½" squares together to make a sashing row. Make two rows that measure 2½" × 52½".

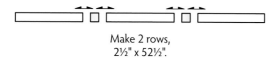

Make 2 rows,
2½" x 52½".

3 Sew the block and sashing rows together in alternating positions. The quilt top should now measure 52½" square, including seam allowances.

Adding the Border

1 Piece the six remaining white 2½" × 42" strips together end to end. From this length, cut two strips, 52½" long, and sew them to the sides of the quilt top.

2 From the remainder of the white strip, cut two strips, 56½" long, and sew them to the top and bottom of the quilt top. The completed quilt top should measure 56½" square.

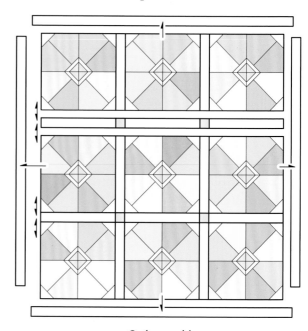

Quilt assembly

Finishing the Quilt

For detailed instructions on any of the finishing steps, go to ShopMartingale.com/HowtoQuilt for free information.

1 Layer the backing, batting, and quilt top; baste.

2 Quilt by hand or machine. This quilt has petals in the block centers and feathers in the print sections of each block. Between the blocks are straight lines that create an X and wreaths of leaves.

3 Use the turquoise 2¼"-wide strips to make the binding; attach it to the quilt.

Pinwheel Flowers

NANCY MAHONEY

E asy patchwork techniques make short work of these tricky-looking blocks. This quilt includes 1930s reproduction fabrics, but imagine this design in a rich assortment of batiks, earth-toned fabrics, or holiday colors. The possibilities are endless!

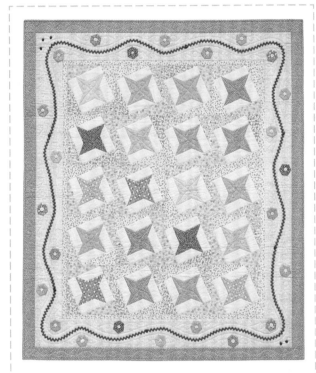

Finished quilt: 46½" × 54½"
Finished block: 8" × 8"

Materials

Yardage is based on 42"-wide fabric. Fat eighths are 9" × 21".

1 fat eighth *each* of 9 assorted medium or dark prints for blocks and folded hexagon flowers (collectively referred to as *dark*)

1 yard of cream solid for blocks

1 fat eighth *each* of 9 assorted light background prints for blocks

⅞ yard of green print for blocks, outer border, and binding

⅓ yard of light floral for blocks and inner border

1½ yards of yellow print for middle border*

3¼ yards of fabric for backing

53" × 61" piece of batting

5 yards of green ½"-wide rickrack for vine

24 yellow buttons, about ½" diameter

Ladybug, bee, or other novelty buttons (optional)

Fabric glue (optional)

*Yardage amount is for one-piece lengthwise-cut borders. If you don't mind seams in your outer border, ⅞ yard is sufficient to cut crosswise strips.

Cutting

All measurements include ¼"-wide seam allowances. Cut all strips across the width of the fabric, unless indicated otherwise.

From *each* of the 9 assorted dark fat eighths, cut:
2 strips, 2" × 21" (18 total)

From the remainder of the assorted dark fat eighths, cut a *total* of:
24 circles (pattern on page 153)

From the cream solid, cut:
14 strips, 2" × 42"; crosscut into:
    20 strips, 2" × 21"
    80 squares, 2" × 2"

From *each* of the assorted light background fat eighths, cut:
2 strips, 3½" × 21"; crosscut into 4 rectangles, 3½" × 8" (36 total)

Continued on page 151

149

Continued from page 149

From the green print, cut:

5 strips, 2¼" × 42"

7 strips, 2" × 42"; crosscut *1* strip into 2 strips, 2" × 21" Set aside the remainder of the strips for the binding.

From the light floral, cut:

1 strip, 3½" × 42"; crosscut into 4 rectangles, 3½" × 8"

4 strips, 1¼" × 42"

From the *lengthwise* grain of the yellow print, cut:

4 strips, 5" × 46" (or 5 strips, 5" × 42", from the crosswise grain)

Making the Blocks

After sewing each seam, press seam allowances in the directions indicated by the arrows.

1 Using the 2"-wide strips, sew a dark or green strip and a cream strip together along their long edges to make a strip set. Make 20 strip sets. Crosscut each strip set into four 3½"-wide segments (80 total). Keep the four matching segments from each strip set together.

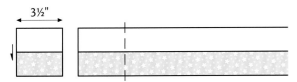

Make 20 strip sets.
Cut 4 segments from each strip set (80 total).

2 Draw a diagonal line on the wrong side of each cream square. Place a cream square on one print corner of a segment from step 1 as shown. Sew along the line and trim away the corner fabric, leaving a ¼" seam allowance. Make 80 units. Keep the matching units together.

Make 4 matching
units (80 total).

3 Lay out four matching units in a four-patch arrangement as shown. Sew the units together into rows, and then sew the rows together. Make 20 star units.

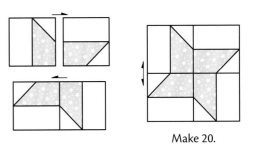

Make 20.

4 With the right side facing up, cut each light 3½" × 8" rectangle diagonally as shown to make 80 long triangles. Make sure you cut each rectangle exactly as shown, or your blocks will tilt in the wrong direction.

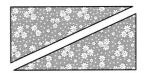

Cut 80 long triangles.

5 Randomly select and sew long triangles to opposite sides of each star unit from step 3, offsetting the triangles ¼" as shown. Sew long triangles to the remaining two sides of the block and press. Make 20 blocks. Trim each block to 8½" square, making sure to leave ¼" beyond the points on all sides for seam allowances.

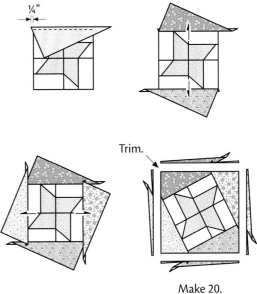

Make 20.

Assembling the Quilt Top

1 Lay out the blocks in five rows of four blocks each. Sew the blocks together into rows and press the seam allowances in opposite directions from row to row. Sew the rows together and press the seam allowances in one direction. The quilt top should measure 32½" × 40½", including seam allowances.

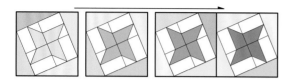

2 Sew the light floral 1¼"-wide strips together end to end. Measure the length of the quilt top through the center. Cut two strips to that measurement and sew them to the sides of the quilt top. Measure the width of the quilt top through the center, including the borders just added. Cut two strips to that measurement and sew them to the top and bottom of the quilt top. The quilt top should now measure 34" × 42", including seam allowances.

3 Repeat step 2 to measure, cut, and sew the yellow 5"-wide strips for the middle border. The quilt top should now measure 43" × 51", including seam allowances.

4 Repeat step 2 to measure, cut, and sew the green 2¼"-wide strips for the outer border.

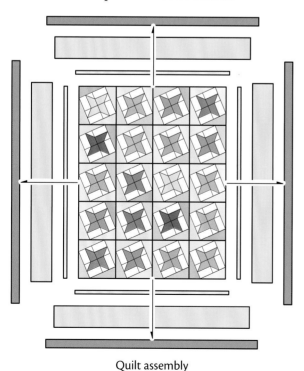

Quilt assembly

5 For the rickrack vine, arrange the green rickrack on the middle border in a meandering line as shown in the photo on page 149. Pin or glue in place, and then use matching thread to topstitch through the center of the rickrack vine.

Finishing the Quilt

For detailed instructions on any of the finishing steps, go to ShopMartingale.com/HowtoQuilt for free information.

1 Layer the backing, batting, and quilt top; baste.

2 Quilt by hand or machine. The quilt shown features loops and wavy lines. See the quilting suggestion below.

Quilting diagram

3 Use the green 2"-wide strips to make the binding; attach it to the quilt.

Adding the Flowers

1 Fold a dark circle into quarters and lightly press to make centering lines. With the wrong side facing up, fold one edge of the circle to the center line as shown and press the fold.

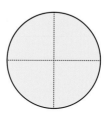

Press.

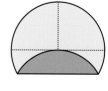

Fold and press.

2 Fold one of the just-created points to the center; press the fold. Continue folding points to the center and pressing to complete a hexagon flower. Make 24 flowers.

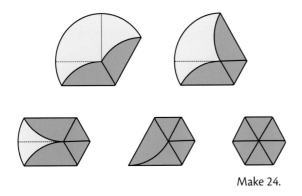

Make 24.

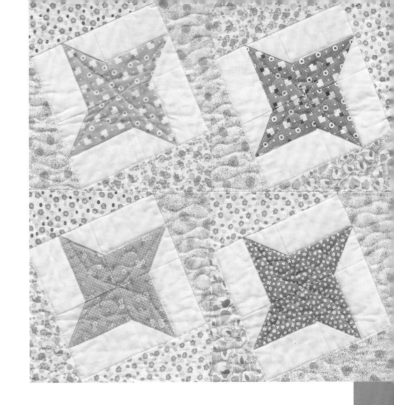

3 After the quilting is completed, arrange the flowers along the rickrack vine as shown in the photo on page 149. Sew a yellow button in the center of each flower, and then sew the flower to the quilt top along the flower's outer edges. Add novelty buttons to the yellow border as desired.

Pattern does not
include seam allowance.

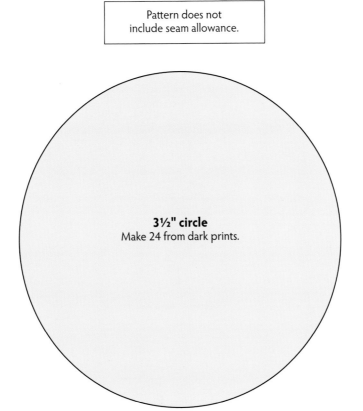

3½" circle
Make 24 from dark prints.

Chocolat et Crème

JOANNA FIGUEROA

Inspired by gorgeous floral fabrics, this quilt flowed naturally from the soft color palette of the fabric itself. To create a similar mood, start with a floral fabric that inspires you, add a few coordinating fabrics, and you will be well on your way to creating your own quilted *crème* masterpiece.

Materials

Yardage is based on 42"-wide fabric.

1 yard of green polka-dot fabric for block star points
3 yards of cream solid for background
1½ yards of small-scale cream print for block centers and outer border
1 yard of chocolate brown floral for large star points and inner border
⅝ yard of fabric for binding
4 yards of fabric for backing
73" × 73" piece of batting

Cutting

All measurements include ¼"-wide seam allowances.

From the green polka-dot fabric, cut:
8 strips, 4" × 42"; crosscut into 72 squares, 4" × 4"

From the cream solid for background, cut:
12 strips, 4" × 42"; crosscut into:
    36 pieces, 4" × 7½"
    36 squares, 4" × 4"
2 strips, 7½" × 42"; crosscut into 4 pieces, 7½" × 14½"
4 strips, 7½" × 42"; crosscut each strip into:
    1 piece, 7½" × 21½" (4 total)
    1 piece, 7½" × 14½" (4 total)

From the small-scale cream print, cut:
2 strips, 7½" × 42"; crosscut into 9 squares, 7½" × 7½"
8 strips, 4" × 42"

From the chocolate brown floral, cut:
2 strips, 7½" × 42"; crosscut into 8 squares, 7½" × 7½"
6 strips, 2½" × 42"

From the binding fabric, cut:
7 strips, 2¼" × 42"

Making the Blocks

After sewing each seam, press seam allowances in the directions indicated by the arrows.

1 Press the green squares in half diagonally, right sides together.

2 Mark a diagonal line from corner to corner on the wrong side of each green 4" square. Place a green square on one end of a cream 4" × 7½" piece, orienting and sewing on the line as shown. Fold over the green piece, aligning the edges, and press. Unfold and trim the seam allowance to ¼". Repeat on the opposite end of the cream piece. Repeat to make a total of 36 flying-geese units.

Make 36.

Finished quilt: 67½" × 67½"
Finished block: 14" × 14"

*Designed and sewn by Joanna Figueroa;
quilted by Diana Johnson*

Fresh Tip

Whenever you're sewing together pieces with points, like these stars, always sew with the "point" piece on top. As you're sewing, you'll be able to see the point and make slight adjustments to your seamline so that you stitch right above the tip—and end up with perfect points. Small adjustments in or out on your sewing line won't affect your block, but this will help you achieve crisp star points every time.

3 Sew a flying-geese unit to the sides of a cream print 7½" square. Join a cream 4" square to the ends of two additional flying-geese units. Sew these units to the top and bottom of the previous unit. Repeat to make a total of nine blocks that measure 14½" square, including seam allowances.

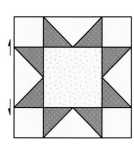
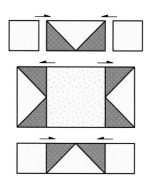

Make 9.

Assembling the Quilt Top

1 Press the chocolate 7½" squares in half diagonally, right sides together. Repeat step 2 of "Making the Blocks" to make four flying-geese units with the folded chocolate squares and four cream 7½" × 14½" pieces.

2 Sew a flying-geese unit to one side of four blocks as shown.

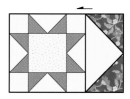

Make 4.

3 Join a cream 7½" × 14½" piece to the left edge of two blocks and then to the right edge of two blocks. Sew a cream 7½" × 21½" piece to the top of these units. Each unit should measure 21½" square, including seam allowances.

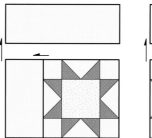
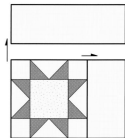

Make 2 of each.

4. Arrange the units from steps 2 and 3 and the remaining block into three vertical rows. Sew the units in each row together. Sew the rows together. The quilt top should measure 56½" square, including seam allowances.

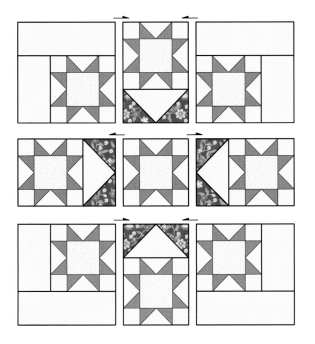

5. Add the chocolate 2½"-wide inner-border strips to the quilt top, piecing as necessary. Repeat with the cream print 4"-wide strips for the outer border.

Finishing the Quilt

For detailed instructions on any of the finishing steps, go to ShopMartingale.com/HowtoQuilt for free information.

1. Layer the backing, batting, and quilt top; baste.

2. Quilt by hand or machine. The quilt shown is quilted with dramatic wreaths and feathers. This type of heirloom quilting really adds to the vintage flavor of a quilt.

3. Use the 2¼"-wide strips to make the binding; attach it to the quilt.

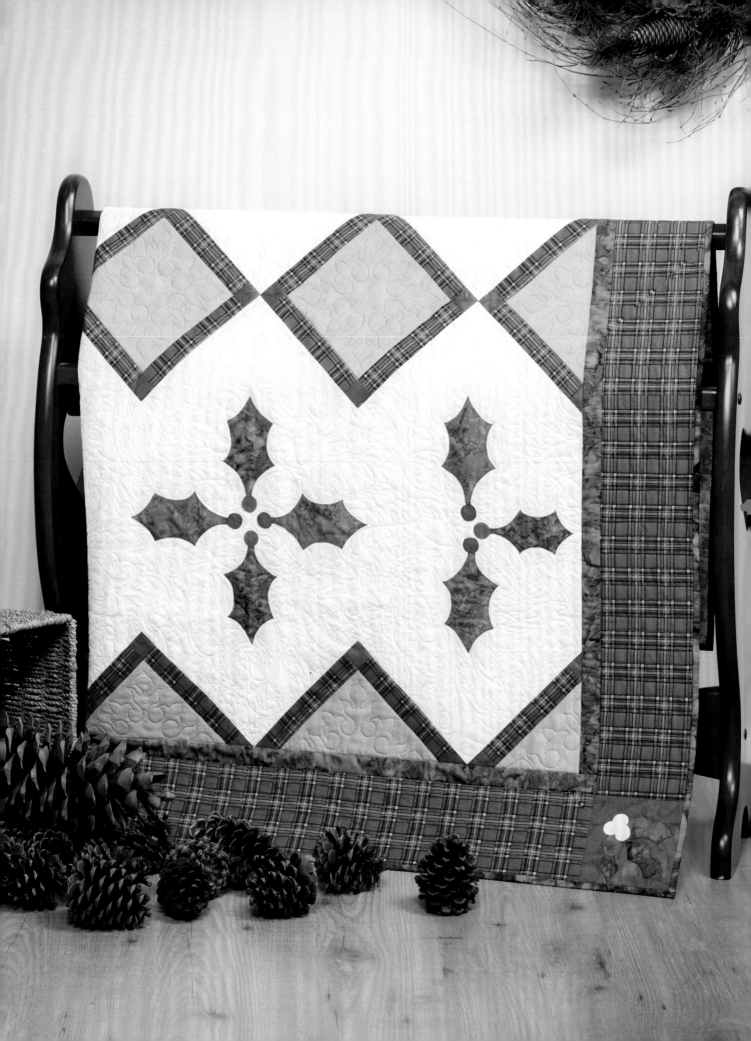

Holly Jolly Christmas Quilt

CHERYL ALMGREN TAYLOR

Combine holiday trappings in a festive quilt you'll be thrilled to bring out year after year. A snow-white background, ribbonlike plaid, and holly appliqués in lifelike shades of red and green let you greet the season with beginner-friendly quilting.

Materials

Yardage is based on 42"-wide fabric.

1½ yards of white tone on tone for appliqué block backgrounds and outer-border berry appliqués

⅜ yard of red batik for berry appliqués, pieced blocks, pieced setting triangles, and outer-border corner blocks

1 yard of red plaid for pieced blocks, pieced setting triangles, and outer border

½ yard of apple-green print for pieced blocks and pieced setting triangles

1 yard of green batik #1 for holly appliqués, inner border, and binding

¼ yard of green batik #2 for holly appliqués

Scrap of red fabric for berry appliqués

2⅞ yards of fabric for backing

52" × 63" piece of batting

1 yard of 17"-wide lightweight paper-backed fusible web

Assorted threads to match appliqué fabrics

Teflon pressing sheet (recommended)

Cutting

All measurements include ¼"-wide seam allowances.

From the white tone on tone, cut:

1 square, 12⅝" × 12⅝"; cut the square into quarters diagonally to yield 4 triangles

16 squares, 9" × 9"

From the red batik, cut:

4 squares, 5½" × 5½"

34 squares, 1½" × 1½"

From the red plaid, cut:

5 strips, 5" × 42"

5 strips, 1½" × 42"; crosscut into 24 rectangles, 1½" × 6½"

From the apple-green print, cut:

1 strip, 9¾" × 42"; crosscut into:

2 squares, 9¾" × 9¾"; cut into quarters diagonally to yield 8 side setting triangles (2 are extra)

2 squares, 6½" × 6½"

2 squares, 5⅛" × 5⅛"; cut the squares in half diagonally to yield 4 corner setting triangles

From green batik #1, cut:

6 strips, 2½" × 42"

5 strips, 1½" × 42"

Finished quilt: 45½" × 56¾"

Pieced and appliquéd by Cheryl Almgren Taylor;
quilted by Cheryl Winslow

Making the Appliquéd Pieces

Preassemble the appliqué units by laying them on the Teflon pressing sheet in numerical order. Remove the paper backing behind only the areas that overlap, not from the entire piece. Fuse the pieces together. Keep the rest of the paper backing in place. Patterns are on pages 163 and 164.

- Preassemble the large and medium holly units, pairing the green #1 leaves with the red batik berries and the green #2 leaves with the red scrap berries.

- Preassemble the border holly units, using white for the berries and a mixture of green leaves for each unit.

1 Position a large holly unit on one corner of each white 9" square using the placement lines. Position a medium holly unit on each white triangle using the

Follow the Lines

It's important to follow the placement lines when positioning the holly units on the white squares and rectangles so there will be a consistent amount of space around them and so that the appliqués won't be caught in the seam allowances.

placement lines. Center a border holly unit on each red batik 5½" square, leaving at least ½" on each side for trimming and seam allowances. Follow the manufacturer's instructions to fuse the units in place.

2 Finish the raw edges of each appliqué piece using a machine blanket stitch, zigzag stitch, or satin stitch.

3 Trim the white 9" blocks to 8½" square, leaving a ¼" seam allowance around the berries. Square up the red 5½" outer-border blocks to 5" square, keeping the appliqué unit centered. Do not trim the white setting triangles.

Making the Pieced Blocks and Setting Triangles

After sewing each seam, press seam allowances in the directions indicated by the arrows.

1 Sew a red batik 1½" square on one end of a red plaid 1½" × 6½" rectangle. Make 20 units. Set aside six of these units and label them unit A. With the remaining 14 units, sew a red 1½" square to the opposite end of the 6½" rectangle. Label these unit B.

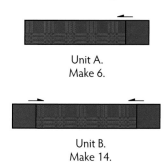

Unit A.
Make 6.

Unit B.
Make 14.

2 Sew red plaid 1½" × 6½" rectangles to opposite sides of each apple-green 6½" square. Add a B unit to the top and bottom of each square.

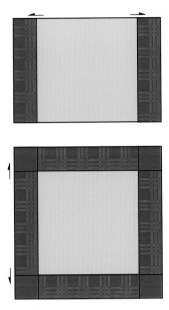

Make 2.

3 Sew an A unit to the short side of each apple-green side setting triangle as shown, making sure the end of the plaid rectangle lines up with the bottom of the triangle. The red square on the end of the A unit will extend past the triangle. On the adjacent short side of each triangle, sew a B unit, aligning the red square on the B unit with the plaid rectangle of the A unit.

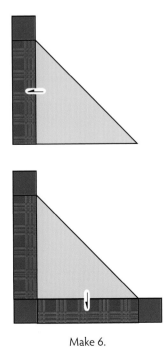

Make 6.

4 Trim the A and B units even with the long diagonal edge of the apple-green triangle, making sure the ¼" line of the ruler is aligned with the diagonal center of the red squares.

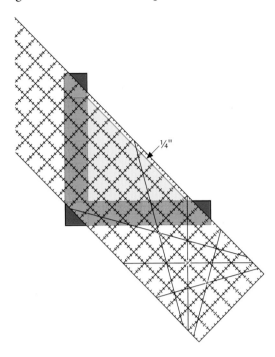

5 To make the pieced corner setting triangles, fold each apple-green corner setting triangle in half along the long edge and crease the fold to find the center. Fold the remaining B units in half crosswise and crease the fold. With the crease marks matching, sew a B unit to the long side of each triangle. Trim the B units even with the short sides of the triangle, making sure the ¼" line of the ruler is aligned with the diagonal center of the red squares.

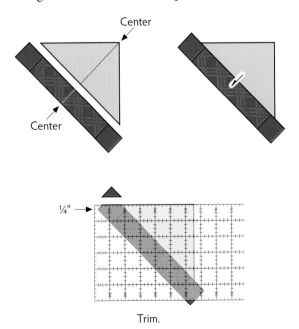

Trim.

Assembling the Quilt Top

1 Refer to the quilt assembly diagram below to arrange the blocks and setting triangles into diagonal rows. Sew the blocks and side setting triangles into rows and press. Press the seam allowances in alternating directions from row to row. Sew the rows together, adding the corner triangles to the quilt top last. The white appliquéd side setting triangles were cut slightly oversized; trim them even with the sides of the quilt top if necessary, being careful to leave ¼" of seam allowance from the point of the holly leaves. Square up the corners of the quilt top as well.

2 Add the 1½"-wide green #1 inner-border strips to the quilt top, piecing the strips as necessary.

3 Measure the length and width of the quilt top through the center and make a note of the measurements. From the red plaid 5"-wide strips, cut two strips to the length measured for the outer-border side strips and two strips to the width

measured for the outer-border top and bottom strips, piecing the strips as needed to achieve the required length. Sew the side borders to the sides of the quilt top. Add an outer-border appliquéd holly block to each end of the outer-border top and bottom strips. Press the seam allowances toward the plaid strips. Join these strips to the top and bottom of the quilt top.

Finishing the Quilt

For detailed instructions on any of the finishing steps, go to ShopMartingale.com/HowtoQuilt for free information.

1 Layer the backing, batting, and quilt top; baste.

2 Quilt by hand or machine. The quilt shown is quilted with a fleur-de-lis design in the pieced blocks and setting triangles. An allover design fills the background.

3 Use the 2½"-wide green #1 strips to make the binding; attach it to the quilt.

Quilt assembly

Appliqué patterns do not
include seam allowances.

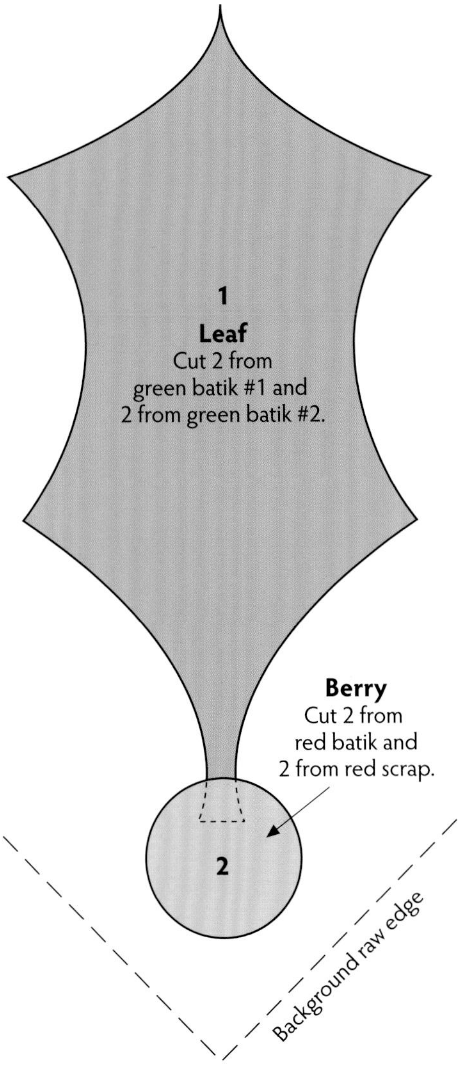

**Large holly appliqué patterns
and placement guide**

**Medium holly appliqué patterns
and placement guide**

1

Leaf
Cut 2 from
green batik #1 and
2 from green batik #2.

1

Leaf
Cut 8 from
green batik #1 and
8 from green batik #2.

Berry
Cut 2 from
red batik and
2 from red scrap.

2

Background raw edge

Berry
Cut 8 from
red batik and
8 from red scrap.

2

Background raw edge

Appliqué patterns do not
include seam allowances.

**Outer-border holly appliqué patterns
and placement guide**

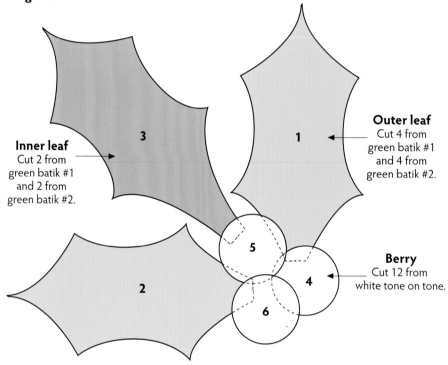

Inner leaf
Cut 2 from
green batik #1
and 2 from
green batik #2.

3

1

Outer leaf
Cut 4 from
green batik #1
and 4 from
green batik #2.

5

4

Berry
Cut 12 from
white tone on tone.

2

6

Four-Patch Log Cabin

SUSAN ACHE

The blocks in this quilt are constructed Courthouse Steps style, and then grouped into four-patch units. As a time-saver, you can use rolls of precut 1½"-wide strips in a variety of prints.

Materials

Yardage is based on 42"-wide fabric.

4 rolls of 40 precut strips, 1½" × 42", for blocks*
2 yards of cream solid for block centers, sashing, and binding
4⅓ yards of fabric for backing
75" × 75" piece of batting

Or 142 strips, 1½" × 42"

Cutting

To make sure you have sufficient fabric for your logs, cut the longest ones first, as listed below. All measurements include ¼"-wide seam allowances.

From the assorted print strips, cut 36 matching sets of:
2 logs, 1½" × 10½", and 2 logs, 1½" × 8½" (round 4)
2 logs, 1½" × 8½", and 2 logs, 1½" × 6½" (round 3)
2 logs, 1½" × 6½", and 2 logs, 1½" × 4½" (round 2)
2 logs, 1½" × 4½", and 2 logs, 1½" × 2½" (round 1)

From the cream solid, cut:
26 strips, 2½" × 42"; crosscut 12 of the strips into:
    12 strips, 2½" × 20½"
    36 squares, 2½" × 2½"

Making the Blocks

After sewing each seam, press seam allowances in the directions indicated by the arrows. In the blocks, press seam allowances away from the center square, toward the log just added.

1 Choose a matching set of four logs for each round.

2 For round 1, sew the 1½" × 2½" logs to opposite sides of a cream 2½" square. Sew the 1½" × 4½" logs to the top and bottom of the unit as shown.

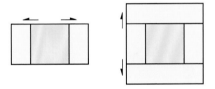

3 For round 2, sew the 1½" × 4½" logs to opposite sides of the unit. Sew the 1½" × 6½" logs to the top and bottom. Continue adding the remaining rounds of logs in the same manner to assemble a block. Make a total of 36 blocks. The blocks should measure 10½" square, including seam allowances.

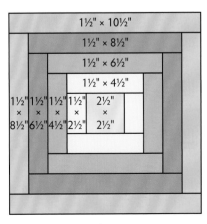

Make 36.

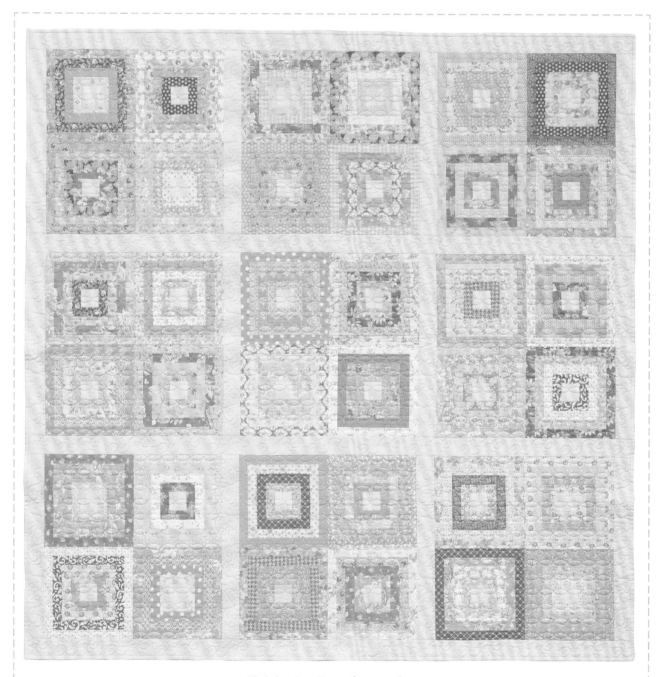

Finished quilt: 68½" × 68½"
Finished block: 10" × 10"

4 Join four blocks to create a four-patch section, rotating the placement of the long outer logs as shown. Make nine four-patch sections.

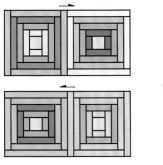
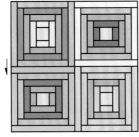

Make 9.

Assembling the Quilt Top

1 Lay out three four-patch sections, adding the cream 2½" × 20½" horizontal sashing strips as shown. Join the four-patch sections to the sashing. Make three columns.

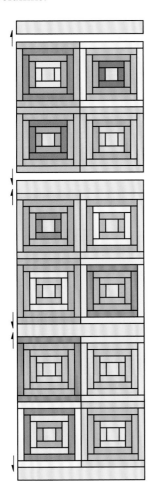

Make 3.

2 Join seven cream 2½" × 42" strips end to end to make one long strip. From this strip, cut four strips, 68½" long, for the vertical sashing.

3 Join the block columns and the cream 2½" × 68½" vertical sashing strips to complete the quilt top as shown.

Quilt assembly

Finishing the Quilt

For detailed instructions on any of the finishing steps, go to ShopMartingale.com/HowtoQuilt for free information.

1 Layer the backing, batting, and quilt top; baste.

2 Quilt by hand or machine. The blocks in this quilt are quilted with overall interlocking circles, creating an orange-peel design. A floral vine motif is quilted in the sashing and border.

3 Use the remaining cream 2½"-wide strips to make the binding; attach it to the quilt.

Finished quilt: 60½" × 76½"

Pieced and machine quilted by Linda Barrett

Jazz

SUSAN GUZMAN

Surround your logs with sashing for a modern take on a Log Cabin block. As with the traditional block, piecing begins in the center. Being organized is important with this quilt because of all the different strip sizes. Labeling each patch and strip you cut is of paramount importance for worry-free piecing. For its designer, this cheerful quilt brings to mind a summertime jazz festival.

Materials

Yardage is based on 42"-wide fabric. Fat quarters are 18" × 21".

16 fat quarters of assorted orange, purple, blue, green, red, yellow, and pink prints for rectangles
3⅜ yards of white solid for sashing, outer border, and binding
5 yards of fabric for backing
68" × 84" piece of batting

Cutting

All measurements include ¼"-wide seam allowances.

From the assorted fat quarters, cut a *total* of:
1 rectangle, 2½" × 12½" (A)
9 rectangles, 4½" × 12½" (E)
17 rectangles, 4½" × 10½" (F)
14 rectangles, 4½" × 8½" (D)
19 rectangles, 4½" × 6½" (C)
21 rectangles, 2½" × 4½" (B)

From the *lengthwise* grain of the white solid, cut:
16 strips, 2½" × 72½"; cut 14 of the strips into:
    1 strip, 2½" × 66½" (Z)
    3 strips, 2½" × 60½" (Y)
    1 strip, 2½" × 56½" (X)
    1 strip, 2½" × 54½" (W)
    1 strip, 2½" × 50½" (V)
    1 strip, 2½" × 48½" (U)
    1 strip, 2½" × 44½" (T)
    1 square, 2½" × 2½" (G)
    1 rectangle, 2½" × 8½" (J)
    1 strip, 2½" × 14½" (K)
    1 strip, 2½" × 42½" (S)
    1 strip, 2½" × 18½" (H)
    1 strip, 2½" × 38½" (R)
    1 strip, 2½" × 20½" (L)
    1 strip, 2½" × 36½" (Q)
    1 strip, 2½" × 24½" (M)
    1 strip, 2½" × 32½" (P)
    1 strip, 2½" × 26½" (N)
    1 strip, 2½" × 30½" (O)

From the *crosswise* grain of the remaining white solid, cut:
4 strips, 4½" × 42"; crosscut into 61 rectangles, 2½" × 4½" (I)
8 strips, 2½" × 42"

Laying Out the Pieces

Lay out the print A–F rectangles, the white G square, and the white H–Z rectangles as shown in the quilt assembly diagram on page 171.

Assembling the Quilt Top

After sewing each seam, press seam allowances in the directions indicated by the arrows.

1 Join the pieces into units, starting in the center of the quilt top with the print A rectangle, the white G square, and a print B rectangle. Sew the white H strip to the right side of the row.

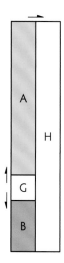

2 Join one print B rectangle, two white I rectangles, and two print C rectangles to make a unit. Sew the row to the other side of the H strip.

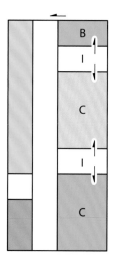

3 Sew the white J rectangle and a print D rectangle to the top of the unit from step 2. Sew the white M strip to the left side of the unit.

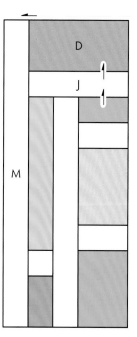

Continue in the same way, joining the rectangles into units, and then sewing the units and white strips to the center unit as shown in the quilt assembly diagram. The quilt center should measure 56½" × 72½", including seam allowances.

Sew the remaining white 72½"-long strips to opposite sides of the quilt center. Press the seam allowances toward the white strips. Sew the remaining Y strips to the top and bottom of the quilt top to complete the border. Press the seam allowances toward the white strips.

Finishing the Quilt

For detailed instructions on any of the finishing steps, go to ShopMartingale.com/HowtoQuilt for free information.

1. Layer the backing, batting, and quilt top; baste.

2. Quilt by hand or machine. The quilt shown is quilted with an allover swirl pattern.

3. Use the white 2½"-wide strips to make the binding; attach it to the quilt.

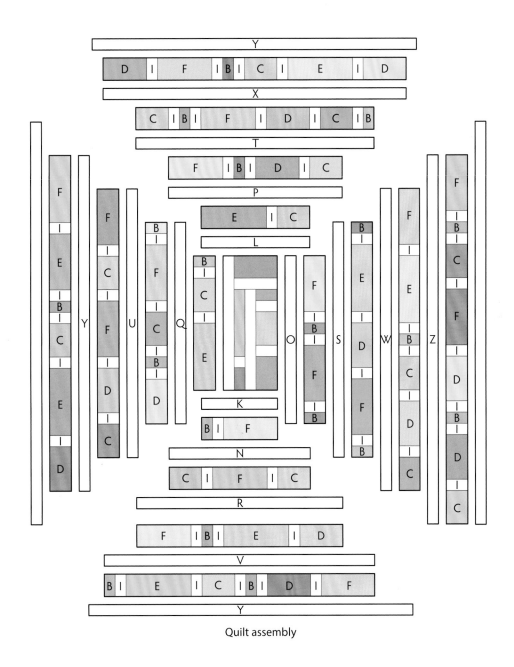

Quilt assembly

Crosswalk

JEANNE LARGE AND SHELLEY WICKS

A welcoming winter project, this is one of those easy quilts that you can make many times over in various colorways. Whether you choose red prints or just use your stash, the end result is an appealing quilt that looks far more complicated than it really is.

Materials

Yardage is based on 42"-wide fabric. Fat quarters are 18" × 21".

14 fat quarters of assorted red prints for blocks
2 yards of beige print for block background
⅝ yard of red print for binding
3⅔ yards of fabric for backing
63" × 77" piece of batting

Cutting

All measurements include ¼"-wide seam allowances.

From *each* of the red fat quarters, cut:
5 strips, 3" × 21"; crosscut the strips into 29 squares, 3" × 3" (406 total; 6 are extra)

From the beige print, cut:
5 strips, 8⅜" × 42"; crosscut the strips into 20 squares, 8⅜" × 8⅜". Cut the squares into quarters diagonally to yield 80 triangles.
5 strips, 4½" × 42"; crosscut the strips into 40 squares, 4½" × 4½". Cut the squares in half diagonally to yield 80 triangles.

From the red print, cut:
7 strips, 2½" × 42"

Making the Blocks

After sewing each seam, press seam allowances in the directions indicated by the arrows.

1 Sew four different red 3" squares together in pairs. Sew the pairs together to make a four-patch unit. Make 100 four-patch units.

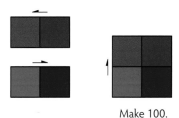

Make 100.

2 Sew three of the four-patch units together. Make 20 of these units.

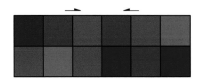

Make 20.

Finished quilt: 56½" × 70½"

Finished block: 14" × 14"

*Designed and pieced by
Jeanne Large and Shelley Wicks;
machine quilted by Wendy Findlay*

4 Lay out two units from step 3 together with a unit from step 2 as shown and sew the units together.

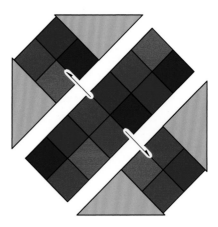

5 Sew a beige 4½" triangle to each corner of the block. The block should measure 14½" square, including seam allowances. Make 20 blocks.

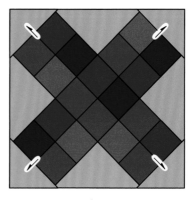

3 Sew beige 8⅜" triangles to opposite sides of the remaining four-patch units. The bottom of the triangle will line up with the bottom of the four-patch unit and the point of the triangle will be slightly longer than the four-patch unit. Make 40 of these units.

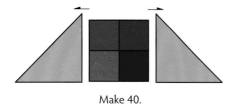

Make 40.

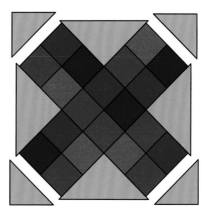

Make 20.

6 Trim each block to measure 14½" square, including seam allowances. Be sure to leave ¼" seam allowance beyond the points so they will match up when you sew the blocks together.

Assembling the Quilt Top

1 Arrange the blocks into five rows of four blocks each as shown. Sew the blocks together, aligning the seams as you sew.

2 Sew the rows together.

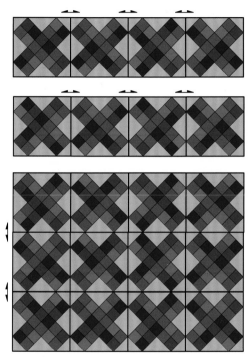

Quilt assembly

Finishing the Quilt

For detailed instructions on any of the finishing steps, go to ShopMartingale.com/HowtoQuilt for free information.

1 Layer the backing, batting, and quilt top; baste.

2 Quilt by hand or machine. The quilt shown is quilted with an allover design.

3 Use the red 2½"-wide strips to make the binding; attach it to the quilt.

Finished quilt: 57½" × 69½"

Finished block: 9" × 9"

Hand Warmers

SUSAN NELSEN

Winter weather calls for mittens to warm fingers while you make snowballs and romp in the snow. Afterwards, curl up by the fireplace with hot cocoa and this quilt. This design will carry you through fall and well into the New Year. The key is the variety of black and white prints contrasted with bright fabrics for mittens. Check your fat-quarter stash, and pore over your button jars for an array of colors and dimensions.

Materials

Yardage is based on 42"-wide fabric. Fat quarters are 18" × 21".

14 fat quarters of assorted black prints for blocks and sashing

8 fat quarters of assorted white prints for sashing and outer border

⅝ yard of black print for binding

1 yard *total* of assorted bright print scraps for mitten appliqués

3⅝ yards of fabric for backing

64" × 76" piece of batting

Template plastic

⅝ yard of fine tulle for the appliqués (optional)

Monofilament for invisible machine appliqué (optional)

120 bright buttons, ½" to ⅞" diameter

96 white buttons, ⅝" diameter

Cutting

All measurements include ¼"-wide seam allowances.

From *each* fat quarter of assorted black prints, cut:

5 strips, 3½" × 21" (70 total; 4 are extra)

From *each* fat quarter of assorted white prints, cut:

3 strips, 2" × 21"; crosscut into 25 squares, 2" × 2" (200 total; 4 are extra)

3 strips, 3½" × 21"; crosscut into 14 squares, 3½" × 3½" (112 total; 2 are extra)

From the black print for binding, cut:

7 strips, 2¾" × 42"

Button Tips

So many buttons, so little time! Instead of sewing on buttons the traditional way, try tying them on with embroidery floss. Use a needle with a large eye to accommodate all six strands of floss, and then take a stitch through the holes of the buttons, leaving tails on the back of the quilt. Tie the ends in a square knot and trim the threads.

Another trick used on this quilt is to stack buttons around the snowflakes. Take a close look and you'll see two buttons were stacked and attached as if they were one button. The bottom button in the stack is ⅝" in diameter. The top button is ¼" in diameter and makes the center of the snowflake. If you stack buttons for your snowflakes, you'll need 96 buttons, ⅝" diameter, and 96 buttons, ¼" diameter. You may discover buttons that complement each other and have different diameters than the ones used here.

Making the Blocks and Sashing

After sewing each seam, press seam allowances in the directions indicated by the arrows.

1 Arrange the 3½"-wide black strips into 22 sets of 3 strips, varying the prints from group to group. You'll have 4 strips left over for another project, but this gives you enough variety to arrange all your sets. Sew each set of 3 strips into a strip set as shown. Press 11 strips sets so that the seam allowances go toward the center, and press the other 11 strip sets so that the seam allowances go toward the outside.

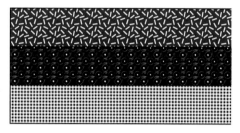

Make 22 strip sets.

2 Cut five 3½" segments from each strip set as shown. You'll have 110 segments, but you'll use only 109.

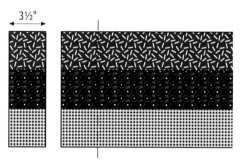

Cut 5 segments from each strip set (110 total).

Piecing the Sashing

1 Using a soft-lead pencil and a see-through ruler, draw a diagonal line from corner to corner on the wrong side of each white 2" square.

2 With right sides together, place the squares on opposite corners of a black segment in which the seam allowances are pressed toward the center, as shown. Stitch on the diagonal lines. Trim ¼" from the stitching lines and press the triangles and their seam allowances toward the corners. Place squares on the remaining corners. Stitch, trim, and press as before. You will have four unused white 2" squares. Be sure

that all the black seam allowances are pressed toward the center. When the quilt has been assembled, all the seam allowances will nest nicely. Make 49 sashing sections.

Make 49 sections.

Making the Mitten Blocks

1 For each Nine Patch block, sew three black segments together, nesting the seam allowances as shown. You may need to re-press some segments so that the seam allowances match the diagram, but if you press as shown, all your seam allowances will nest when you add the sashing, and your quilt will lie neatly flat. The blocks should measure 9½" square, including seam allowances.

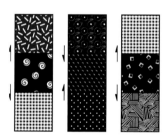 

Make 20.

2 Using the pattern on page 181 and your favorite appliqué method, cut and appliqué 20 pairs of mittens to the Nine Patch blocks. Whatever appliqué method you choose, be sure to position the mittens at least ½" from the edges of the block. See "Invisible Machine Appliqué" on page 179 for instructions.

Make 20.

Especially if you don't have a lot of appliqué experience, this method is an easy way to achieve a turned edge for the appliqués. It also allows you to use an invisible stitch without all the handwork.

1 Trace the appliqué pattern on page 181 onto template plastic and cut out your template.

2 Trace the template onto the wrong side of a bright print and then cut out the mitten shape on the drawn line. Cut one regular and one reversed mitten from each fabric so that you have 20 matching pairs.

3 Cut the fine tulle into 20 rectangles, 4¼" × 5¾". Center a mitten, right side down, over the tulle. Pin the layers together, and using a straight stitch, carefully stitch all the way around the mitten using a scant ¼" seam. Between the mitten and the thumb, clip the V in the seam allowance.

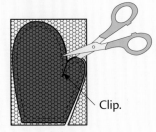

Clip.

4 In the middle of the mitten, cut a slash only through the tulle layer so that you can turn the appliqué shape right side out. From the cotton side, gently press the edges so that the seam allowances lie neatly flat. The tulle is the trick to turning and holding the appliqué edges in this method!

5 Attach an open-toe appliqué foot to your machine. Thread it with monofilament in the top, and in the bobbin, use cotton thread that matches your background. Set your machine to the blind hem stitch, with the stitch size set about 1 mm long and 1 mm wide. You may need to adjust the stitch length and width until you find what works the best for you. Do some practicing before stitching your project.

6 Place a pair of mittens on a Nine Patch block, right sides up, and at least ½" from the edges of the block. Position an appliqué under the presser foot. You want the right swing of your stitch to pierce the background next to the appliqué and the left swing to catch the appliqué. Stitch around the mitten, overlapping the starting point by a few stitches to secure.

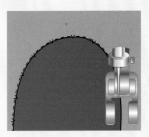

Left swing position

Right swing position

7 To reduce bulk, cut away the background fabric behind the appliqué. Use small, sharp scissors and work from the back of the block. Trim away only the background layer, leaving a seam allowance about ¼"-wide inside the stitching line.

Assembling the Quilt Top

1 For each sashing row, arrange four pieced sashing sections between five white 3½" squares as shown. Sew the pieces together.

Make 6 sashing rows.

2 For each mitten row, arrange four Mitten blocks between five sashing sections as shown. Sew the rows together.

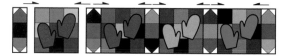

Make 5 block rows.

3 Arrange the mitten rows between the sashing rows. Join the rows and press toward the mitten rows. The quilt top should measure 51½" × 63½", including seam allowances.

4 For each side border, join 21 white 3½" squares and press the seam allowances so that they will nest with the quilt-center seam allowances. Add the side borders to the center. For the top and bottom borders, join 19 white 3½" squares for each border. (You will have two 3½" squares left over.) Again, press the seam allowances so that they will nest with the seam allowances in the quilt center. Sew the borders to the top and bottom of the quilt center.

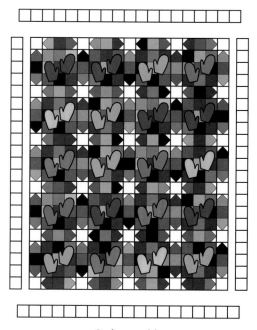

Quilt assembly

Finishing the Quilt

For detailed instructions on any of the finishing steps, go to ShopMartingale.com/HowtoQuilt for free information.

1 Layer the backing, batting, and quilt top; baste.

2 Quilt by hand or machine. The quilt shown is quilted with an allover swirl pattern.

3 Use the black 2¾"-wide strips to make the binding; attach it to the quilt.

4 Embellish the mittens with your collection of bright buttons. Place them as shown in the photo on page 176 or create your own scheme. Then add the white buttons to embellish the snowflakes.

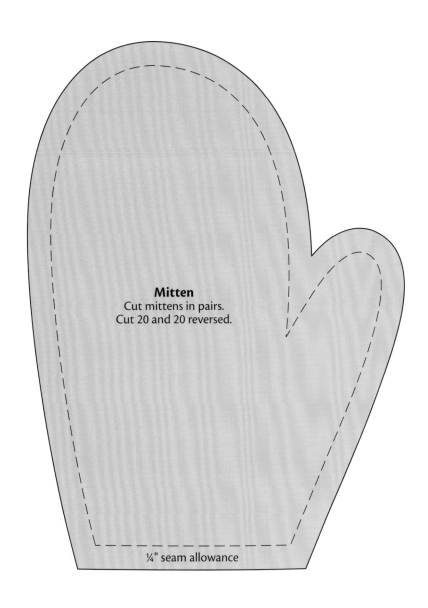

Mitten
Cut mittens in pairs.
Cut 20 and 20 reversed.

¼" seam allowance

Cozy Home Lane

KIM DIEHL

Build your very own charming neighborhood when you piece these sweet little row houses that are so reminiscent of your grandmother's era. Add a sprinkling of patchwork stars for some welcoming ambience, and then embrace your inner homebody as you settle in for some quality quiet time.

Materials

Yardage is based on 42"-wide fabric. Fat quarters are 18" × 21". Chubby sixteenths are 9" × 11".

8 fat quarters of assorted tan prints for patchwork blocks
6 fat quarters of assorted brown prints for House blocks and binding
24 chubby sixteenths of assorted prints for House blocks
4 chubby sixteenths of assorted black prints for House blocks
6 squares, 5½" × 5½", of assorted prints for Star block center squares
48 squares, 3" × 3", of assorted prints for Star block points (scraps equivalent to approximately ¼ yard)
3¾ yards of fabric for backing
63" × 67" rectangle of batting
Acrylic ruler

Cutting

All measurements include ¼"-wide seam allowances.

From *each* of the assorted tan print fat quarters, cut:
2 strips, 2" × 22" (combined total of 16)
6 squares, 4½" × 4½" (combined total of 48)

From the remainder of the assorted tan print fat quarters, cut a *total* of:
24 squares, 3" × 3"
24 rectangles, 3" × 5½"

From *each* of the assorted brown print fat quarters, cut:
4 rectangles, 4½" × 10½" (total of 24)
2 strips, 2½" × 22" (total of 12 for binding)

From *each* of the assorted print chubby sixteenths, cut:
1 rectangle, 2½" × 10½" (total of 24)
2 squares, 4½" × 4½" (total of 48)
Keep the pieces organized by print for the House blocks.

From *each* of the assorted black print chubby sixteenths, cut:
6 rectangles, 2½" × 4½" (total of 24)

Piecing the House Blocks

Sew all pieces with right sides together. After sewing each seam, press seam allowances in the directions indicated by the arrows.

1 Use a pencil and an acrylic ruler to draw a diagonal line on the wrong side of each assorted tan print 4½" square.

2 Select two prepared 4½" squares from different tan prints and one brown 4½" × 10½" rectangle. Layer a tan square over each end of the brown rectangle as shown. Stitch the pairs together on the drawn lines. Press and trim as instructed in "Pressing Triangle Units" on page 184. Repeat for a total of 24 pieced roof units.

Make 24.

Finished quilt: 56½" × 60½"
Finished block: 10" × 10"

*Designed by Kim Diehl; pieced by Pat Peyton;
machine quilted by Deborah Poole*

3 Select a matching set of assorted print pieces to make the base for a House block and select one black 2½" × 4½" rectangle for the door. Join the 4½" assorted print squares to opposite long sides of the black rectangle. Join the 2½" × 10½" assorted print rectangle to the top of the pieced door unit. Repeat for a total of 24 pieced house base units measuring 6½" × 10½", including seam allowances.

Make 24.

4 Join a roof unit to a house base unit. Repeat for a total of 24 House blocks measuring 10½" square, including seam allowances.

Make 24.

5 Lay out six House blocks to make a row. Join the blocks. Repeat for a total of four pieced House strips measuring 10½" × 60½", including seam allowances.

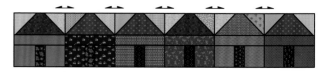

Make 4.

Pressing Triangle Units

Unless otherwise instructed, after stitching the pair of squares together on the drawn line, use the following steps.

1 Fold the top triangle back and align its corner with the corner of the bottom piece of fabric to keep it square; press in place.

2 Trim away the excess layers of fabric beneath the top triangle, leaving a ¼" seam allowance.

The seam allowances of triangle units are commonly trimmed before they are pressed, but this pressing method produces accurate patchwork that seldom requires squaring up.

Piecing the Sidewalk Units

1   Select two different tan 2" × 22" strips. Join the strips along the long sides. Repeat for a total of eight strip sets measuring 3½" × 22". Crosscut the strip sets into a total of 24 segments, 5½" wide.

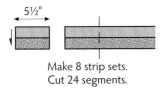

Make 8 strip sets.
Cut 24 segments.

2   Join two different strip-set segments end to end. Repeat for a total of 12 pieced sidewalk units.

Make 12.

3   Referring to the quilt assembly diagram on page 186, lay out six pieced sidewalk units end to end. Join the units. Repeat for a total of two pieced sidewalk strips measuring 3½" × 60½", including seam allowances.

Piecing the Star Blocks

1   Use a pencil and an acrylic ruler to draw a diagonal line on the wrong side of each assorted print 3" square.

2   Select one of the assorted print 5½" squares, eight prepared assorted print 3" squares, four assorted tan 3" × 5½" rectangles, and four assorted tan 3" squares. Layer a prepared assorted print 3" square over one end of a tan 3" × 5½" rectangle. Stitch the pairs together on the drawn line. Press and trim. In the same manner, layer, stitch, press, and trim a second prepared assorted print 3" square onto the remaining end of the pieced rectangle, positioning the square to make a mirror-image point. Repeat for a total of four pieced star-point units.

Make 4.

3   Join a pieced star-point unit to opposite sides of the assorted print 5½" square.

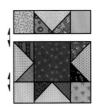

4   Join a tan 3" square to each end of the remaining star-point units.

5   Lay out the center square unit from step 3 and the star-point units from step 4 in three horizontal rows as shown. Join the rows.

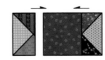

6   Repeat steps 2–5 for a total of six pieced Star blocks measuring 10½" square, including seam allowances.

7   Lay out the Star blocks to make a row. Join the blocks. The pieced Star block strip should measure 10½" × 60½", including seam allowances.

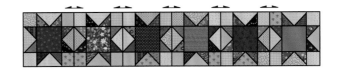

Assembling the Quilt Top

1 Referring to the quilt assembly diagram below, join a pieced House block strip to each long side of a pieced sidewalk strip. Repeat for a total of two pieced House units.

2 Join a pieced House unit to each long side of the pieced Star block strip. The quilt top should now measure 56½" × 60½".

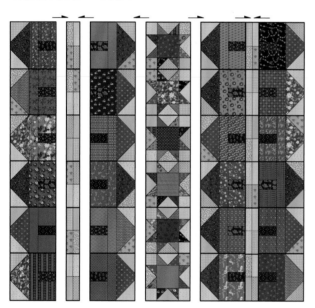

Quilt assembly

Finishing the Quilt

For detailed instructions on any of the finishing steps, go to ShopMartingale.com/HowtoQuilt for free information.

1 Layer the backing, batting, and quilt top; baste.

2 Quilt by hand or machine. The quilt shown is quilted with a crosshatch design on the roofs, Xs in the doorways, and both vertical and horizontal lines on the houses to resemble clapboard siding. An egg-and-dart design is stitched along the sidewalk patchwork, and the Star block centers are crosshatched, with triangular straight lines in the points. The open sky areas are quilted with a small-scale stipple design.

3 Use the assorted brown 2½"-wide strips to make the binding; attach it to the quilt.

It's Cold Outside

JEANNE LARGE AND SHELLEY WICKS

It can be cold outside for several months of the year, so a pair of fuzzy, warm mittens is an important item in everyone's winter wardrobe! Rickrack strings are just the ticket to keep those pairs together.

Finished quilt: 56½" × 56½"
Finished block: 20" × 20"

Designed and made by
Jeanne Large and Shelley Wicks;
machine quilted by Wendy Findlay

Materials

Yardage is based on 42"-wide fabric. Fat eighths are 9" × 21".

3 fat eighths of assorted red flannels for blocks
4 fat eighths of assorted green flannels for blocks
3 fat eighths of assorted blue flannels for blocks
1⅝ yards of light gray flannel for appliqué background and outer border
½ yard of gray flannel for sashing

1 yard of black flannel for inner border and binding
7" × 11" piece *each* of 2 red flannels for mittens and cuffs
7" × 11" piece of green flannel for mittens and cuffs
7" × 11" piece of blue flannel for mittens and cuffs
6" × 18" piece of gold flannel for stars
8" × 8" piece of black flannel for circle
3⅔ yards of fabric for backing
64" × 64" piece of batting
2¾ yards of ⅜"-wide black rickrack
2½ yards of 1½"-wide red rickrack
1 yard of 18"-wide lightweight fusible web
Matching thread for appliqué

Cutting

All measurements include ¼"-wide seam allowances.

From *each* of the red, green, and blue fat eighths, cut:
2 strips, 3½" × 21" (20 total); crosscut the strips into 8 rectangles, 3½" × 4½" (80 total)

From the light gray flannel, cut:
2 strips, 8½" × 42"; crosscut the strips into 4 strips, 8½" × 20½"
6 strips, 4½" × 42"

From the gray flannel, cut:
3 strips, 4½" × 42"; crosscut the strips into:
    4 strips, 4½" × 20½"
    1 square, 4½" × 4½"

From the black flannel, cut:
11 strips, 2½" × 42"

Assembling the Quilt Top

After sewing each seam, press seam allowances in the directions indicated by the arrows.

1 Arrange 20 red, green, and blue 3½" × 4½" rectangles in five rows of four rectangles each. Sew the rectangles together into rows. Sew the rows together to make a section that measures 12½" × 20½", including seam allowances. Make four sections.

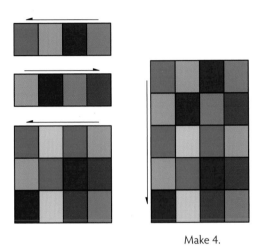

Make 4.

2 Cut the black rickrack into four pieces, 24" long. Referring to "Using Rickrack" at right, position one length of rickrack on a light gray 8½" × 20½" rectangle as shown, forming a gentle loop. Pin in place and then sew the rickrack down. Make four.

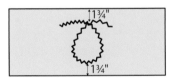

Make 4.

3 Position the red rickrack in a straight line through the center of a gray 4½" × 20½" strip. Sew the rickrack along both edges. Make four sashing strips.

Make 4.

Using Rickrack

Rickrack makes a wonderful vine, flower stem, or accent on a quilt. It comes in a variety of widths and a wide range of colors, so you have plenty of options.

You also have several options when sewing rickrack to your project. If you're using a narrow product, just pin the rickrack in place and sew through the center of the strip by machine. It's a good idea to use a walking foot for doing this to avoid stretching the rickrack. If you're using wide rickrack, sew the edges down on both sides so they won't roll up or distort in any way when your quilt is washed. Sew the edges using a machine blanket stitch or a straight stitch, or drop your feed dogs and free-motion stitch the edges with matching thread.

4 Using your favorite appliqué method and the patterns on page 191, prepare the following from the 7" × 11" pieces of flannel:

- 1 mitten and 1 reversed from each red flannel
- 2 cuffs from each red flannel
- 1 mitten and 1 reversed from green flannel
- 2 cuffs from green flannel
- 1 mitten and 1 reversed from blue flannel
- 2 cuffs from blue flannel
- 8 small stars and 1 large star from gold flannel
- 1 circle from black flannel

5 Arrange the mittens, cuffs, and stars onto each light gray rectangle as shown. Fuse in place. Use matching thread to blanket stitch around each shape by hand or machine.

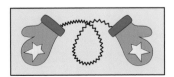

Appliqué placement

Adding the Borders

1 Sew five of the black 2½" × 42" strips end to end to make one long continuous strip. From this strip, cut two strips, 2½" × 44½", and two strips, 2½" × 48½". Sew the 44½"-long strips to opposite sides of the quilt top. Sew the 48½"-long strips to the top and bottom of the quilt top.

2 Sew the light gray 4½" × 42" strips end to end to make one long continuous strip. From this strip, cut two strips, 4½" × 48½", and two strips, 4½" × 56½". Sew the 48½"-long strips to opposite sides of the quilt. Sew the 56½"-long strips to the top and bottom of the quilt.

6 Sew a mitten rectangle to a pieced section as shown. Make four sections.

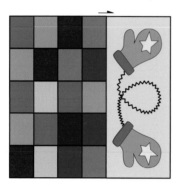

Make 4.

7 Lay out the four sections from step 6 with four sashing strips and the gray 4½" square, rotating each section a quarter turn as shown. Sew the sections and sashing strips together in rows. Sew the sashing strips to each end of the gray center square. Sew the rows together. The quilt top should measure 44½" square, including seam allowances.

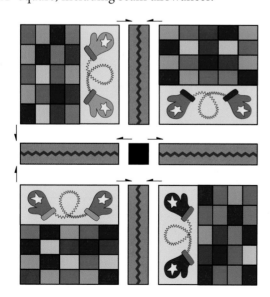

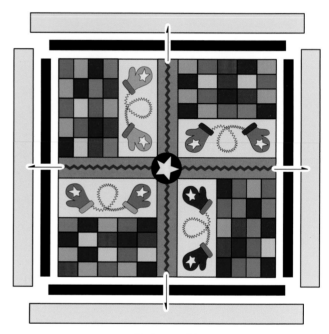

Quilt assembly

Finishing the Quilt

For detailed instructions on any of the finishing steps, go to ShopMartingale.com/HowtoQuilt for free information.

1 Layer the backing, batting, and quilt top; baste.

2 Quilt as desired. The quilt shown is quilted with an allover swirl design.

3 Use the remaining black 2½"-wide strips to make the binding; attach it to the quilt.

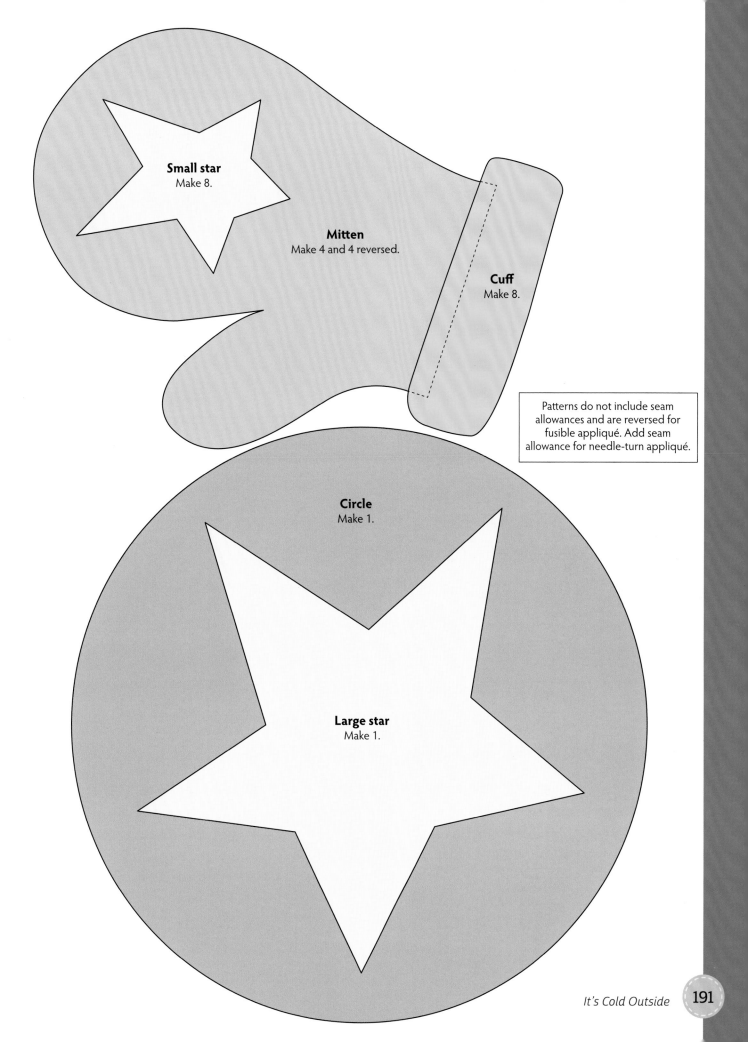

Small star
Make 8.

Mitten
Make 4 and 4 reversed.

Cuff
Make 8.

Patterns do not include seam
allowances and are reversed for
fusible appliqué. Add seam
allowance for needle-turn appliqué.

Circle
Make 1.

Large star
Make 1.

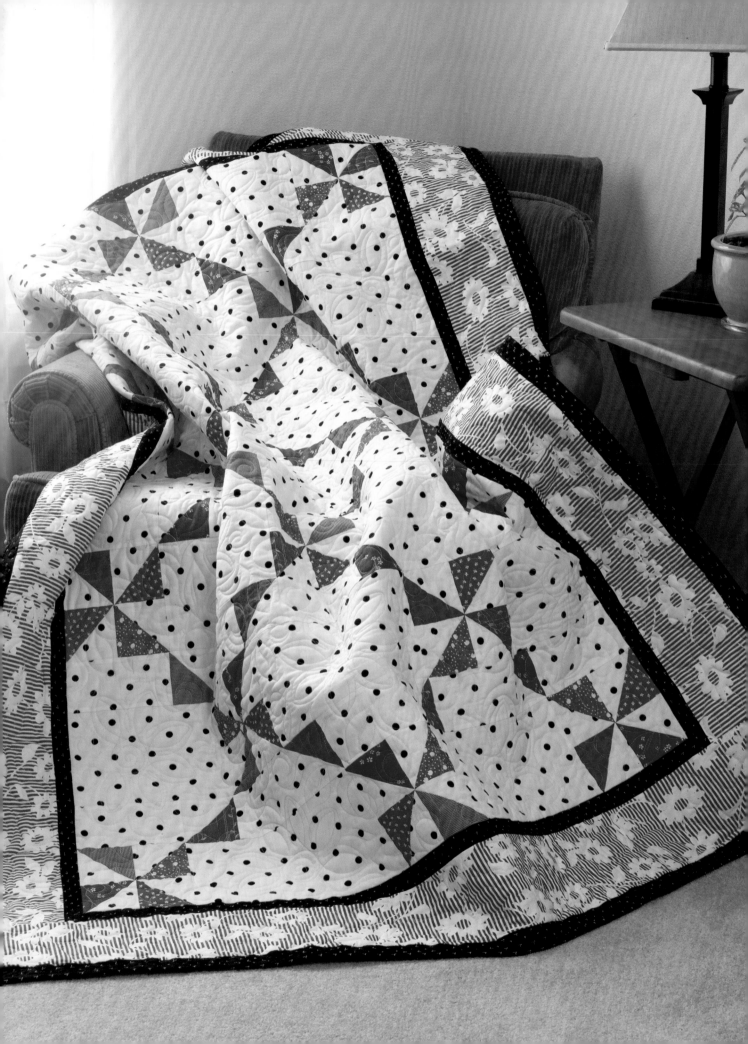

Winding Down

JILL FINLEY

Invite the feeling of fun into your home with this bold and cheery quilt. The design evokes thoughts of leisurely hours spent playing board games, having long conversations, and watching ball games with friends and family. Put this quilt together in a weekend and be ready for your next get-together, where you can relax and wind down from your busy week.

Materials

Yardage is based on 42"-wide fabric.

2½ yards of cream dotted print for blocks and sashing

⅔ yard *total* of assorted red prints for blocks and sashing

1⅛ yards of black print for inner border, outer border, and binding

1⅛ yards of red floral for middle border

3½ yards of fabric for backing

63" × 81" piece of batting

Cutting

From the cream dotted print, cut:

5 strips, 4" × 42"; crosscut into 48 squares, 4" × 4"

9 strips, 6½" × 42"; crosscut into:

    11 rectangles, 6½" × 12½"

    6 rectangles, 6½" × 9½"

    30 rectangles, 3½" × 6½"

From the assorted red prints, cut a *total* of:

5 strips, 4" × 42"; crosscut into 48 squares, 4" × 4"

From the black print, cut:

13 strips, 1½" × 42"

7 strips, 2¼" × 42"

From the red floral, cut:

6 strips, 5½" × 42"

Piecing the Blocks

After sewing each seam, press seam allowances in the directions indicated by the arrows.

1 Draw a diagonal line from corner to corner on the wrong side of each cream 4" square. Place a marked square on top of a red print 4" square, right sides together. Sew ¼" from both sides of the marked line. Cut the squares apart on the marked line to make two half-square-triangle units. Trim the units to 3½" × 3½". Repeat to make a total of 96 half-square-triangle units.

Make 96.

2 Sew two half-square-triangle units together as shown, nesting the seam allowances so the points meet exactly. Repeat to make a total of 12 pairs. Press the seam allowances of each pair in the same direction.

Make 12.

Finished quilt: 56½" × 74½"

Finished block: 6" × 6"

Pieced by Jill Finley;
quilted by Maika Christensen

 Join two pairs from step 2 to make a clockwise-spinning Pinwheel block. Repeat to make a total of six blocks. To press, remove the stitching in the seam allowances at the center of the block, and press the seam allowances in opposite directions so they spiral around the center and lie flat. The blocks should measure 6½" square, including seam allowances.

Clockwise Pinwheel block.
Make 6.

Remove stitching
above cross seam.

Back of block

Repeat steps 2 and 3 with four of the remaining half-square-triangle units, orienting the units so that the pinwheels rotate counterclockwise as shown. Repeat to make a total of 12 counterclockwise Pinwheel blocks. Press the seam allowances as described in step 3.

Counterclockwise Pinwheel block.
Make 12.

Assembling the Quilt Top

Alternately lay out three counterclockwise-spinning Pinwheel blocks along with two cream 6½" × 12½" rectangles. Sew the pieces together to make block row A. Repeat to make a total of four rows. The rows should measure 6½" × 42½", including seam allowances.

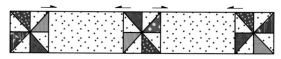

Block row A.
Make 4.

2 Lay out two clockwise-spinning Pinwheel blocks, one cream 6½" × 12½" rectangle, and two cream 6½" × 9½" rectangles as shown. Sew the pieces together to make block row B. Repeat to make a total of three rows. The rows should measure 6½" × 42½", including seam allowances.

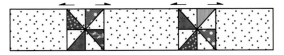

Block row B.
Make 3.

3 Lay out five cream 3½" × 6½" rectangles and four half-square-triangle units as shown. Sew the pieces together to make a sashing row. Repeat to make a total of six rows. The rows should measure 3½" × 42½", including seam allowances.

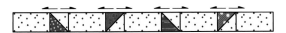

Sashing row.
Make 6.

4 Refer to the quilt assembly diagram below to lay out the block rows and sashing rows, rotating every other sashing row to create the pattern. Sew the rows together. The quilt top should measure 42½" × 60½", including seam allowances.

5 Join the black 1½" × 42" strips end to end to make one long strip. From the pieced strip, cut two 60½"-long strips and two 44½"-long strips for the inner border. Set the remainder of the black strip aside. Sew the 60½"-long inner-border strips to the sides of the quilt center. Sew the 44½"-long inner-border strips to the top and bottom of the quilt center.

6 Join the red floral 5½" × 42" strips end to end to make one long strip. From the pieced strip, cut two 62½"-long strips and two 54½"-long strips for the middle border. Sew the 62½"-long strips to the sides of the quilt top. Sew the 54½"-long strips to the top and bottom of the quilt top.

7 From the remainder of the pieced black strip, cut two 72½"-long strips and two 56½"-long strips

for the outer border. Sew the 72½"-long strips to the sides of the quilt top. Sew the 56½"-long strips to the top and bottom of the quilt top.

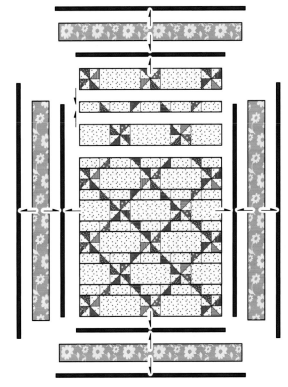

Quilt assembly

Finishing the Quilt

For detailed instructions on any of the finishing steps, go to ShopMartingale.com/HowtoQuilt for free information.

1 Layer the backing, batting (this quilt uses wool batting), and quilt top; baste.

2 Quilt by hand or machine. The quilt shown is quilted with an allover pattern of petals and swirls.

3 Use the black 2¼"-wide strips to make the binding; attach it to the quilt.

Opening Day

CARRIE NELSON

Want to size up or down? Adding a row of stars along one edge of the quilt top will change the dimension of the quilt by 8". Just remember to add eight flying-geese units and two Cotton Reel blocks for each row of Star blocks added. And, if you add a row to the top or bottom and a row to one side, you'll need an additional 16 flying geese and four Cotton Reel blocks. You can also attach an additional border made up of 4" squares or a plain fabric border.

Materials

Yardage is based on 42"-wide fabric. Fat quarters are 18" × 21".

19 fat quarters of assorted blue prints for blocks and flying-geese units

14 fat quarters *OR* 3½ yards *total* of assorted light prints for blocks and flying-geese units

¾ yard of navy print for binding

5 yards of fabric for backing

81" × 81" piece of batting

Cutting

All measurements include ¼"-wide seam allowances.

From *each* blue print, cut:

1 strip, 5¼" × 21" (19 total); crosscut into:
    2 squares, 5¼" × 5¼" (38 total; 6 are extra)
    2 squares, 4⅞" × 4⅞" (38 total; 10 are extra)
    Trim the extra 5¼" and 4⅞" squares to 4½" × 4½" (16 total)

2 strips, 2⅞" × 21" (38 total); crosscut into 8 squares, 2⅞" × 2⅞" (152 total; 8 are extra)

1 strip, 4½" × 21" (19 total); crosscut into 4 squares, 4½" × 4½" (76 total)

From *each* of the assorted light prints, cut:

1 strip, 5¼" × 21" (14 total); crosscut into:
    3 squares, 5¼" × 5¼" (42 total; 6 are extra. Trim 5 of the extra 5¼" squares into 20 squares, 2½" × 2½".)
    2 squares, 2½" × 2½" (28 total)

1 strip, 5¾" × 21" (14 total); crosscut into:
    1 rectangle, 5¾" × 10"; cut the rectangle into 2 squares, 4⅞" × 4⅞" (28 total)
    2 rectangles, 2⅞" × 9"; cut the rectangles into 6 squares, 2⅞" × 2⅞" (84 total; 12 are extra)

1 strip, 2⅞" × 21" (14 total); crosscut into 4 squares, 2⅞" × 2⅞" (56 total)

1 strip, 2½" × 21" (14 total); crosscut into 8 squares, 2½" × 2½" (112 total)

From the navy print, cut:

310" of 2"-wide bias binding

Making the Star Blocks

Press all seam allowances in the directions indicated by the arrows. Use a scant ¼" seam allowance throughout this project. For each block, you'll need the following pieces:

- **Blue:** four matching 2⅞" squares and one 4½" square (or two sets of two matching 2½" squares)

- **Light:** four 2½" squares and one 5¼" square, all matching

Finished quilt: 72½" × 72½"

Finished blocks: 8" × 8"

A Few Words about Pressing

Many of the seam allowances in this quilt were pressed open. The points were sharper, and there wasn't a lot of bulk when the points of the adjacent stars were joined. Most of us learned that seam allowances are never pressed open; they are always pressed to one side. However, that school of thought has changed. The fabrics we use today are better, as is the quality of our thread and batting, and since most of us use sewing machines, the stitches are smaller and tighter. Consequently, fewer issues arise when seam allowances are pressed open. But, in the end, it's entirely a personal choice. A caveat worth considering, if you plan to quilt in the ditch or near the seamline: pressing seam allowances open will make quilting more difficult.

1 On the wrong side of each blue 2⅞" square, draw a diagonal line from corner to corner using a permanent pen, pencil, or chalk marker.

2 With right sides together, place two marked squares on opposite corners of a light 5¼" square as shown. The points of the small squares will overlap a little bit, and the drawn line should extend across the large square from corner to corner.

3 Stitch a scant ¼" from both sides of the drawn line and press. Cut the squares apart on the drawn line.

4 With right sides together, place a remaining marked blue square on the corner of both pieces. The drawn line should extend from the point of the corner to the point between the two small triangles. Stitch a scant ¼" from both sides of the drawn line. Cut the unit apart on the drawn line. The flying-geese units should measure 2½" × 4½". Make 36 sets of four matching units (144 total).

Make 144.

5 Lay out four light 2½" squares, four flying-geese units, and one blue 4½" square in three rows as shown. Sew the pieces together into rows. Join the rows to make a Star block. The block should measure 8½" square, including seam allowances. Make a total of 36 blocks.

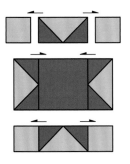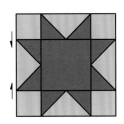

Make 36.

Making the Flying-Geese Strips

For each set of four matching flying-geese units, you'll need the following:

- **Blue:** one 5¼" square
- **Light:** four matching 2⅞" squares

1 Referring to steps 1–4 of "Making the Star Blocks," use a blue 5¼" square and four matching light 2⅞" squares to make four matching flying-geese units. The flying-geese units should measure 2½" × 4½", including seam allowances. Make 32 sets of four matching units (128 total).

Make 128.

2 Divide the units into four groups of 32 geese each. As there are four matching units from each fabric combination, the easiest way to divide the geese would be one from each combination.

3 Using 24 flying-geese units from one group, sew the units together as shown. The strip should measure 4½" × 48½", including seam allowances. Make four 24-unit strips.

Make 4.

4 Use the remaining eight units from each group to make two four-unit strips as shown. Each strip should measure 4½" × 8½", including seam allowances. Make a total of eight four-unit strips.

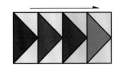

Make 8.

Making the Cotton Reel Blocks

For each block, you'll need the following pieces:

- **Blue:** one 4⅞" square and two different 4½" squares
- **Light:** one 4⅞" square

1 Draw a diagonal line from corner to corner on the wrong side of a light 4⅞" square using a permanent pen, pencil, or chalk marker. Layer a marked square and a blue 4⅞" square, right sides together, and align the raw edges. Stitch a scant ¼" from both sides of the drawn line. Cut the squares apart on the drawn line to make two half-square-triangle units that measure 4½" square. Make a total of 56 units.

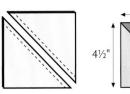

4½"

4½"

Make 56.

Collapsing Seam Allowances

This is one of Carrie's favorite little tricks. It can be used on four-patch units, quarter-square-triangle units, or any block that has four seams intersecting at the center. Use a seam ripper to remove two or three stitches from the seam allowance on both sides of the center seam as shown.

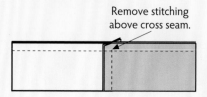

Remove stitching above cross seam.

On the wrong side of the unit or block, open the seam and gently reposition the seam allowance to evenly distribute the fabrics. Press the seam allowances in opposite directions so the center lies flat. When you look at the wrong side of the unit or block, the seam allowances should all be going either clockwise or counterclockwise around the center.

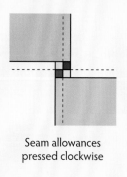

Seam allowances pressed clockwise

2 Lay out two blue 4½" squares and two half-square-triangle units as shown. Sew the pieces together into rows. Join the rows to make a Cotton Reel block. The block should measure 8½" square, including seam allowances. Make a total of 28 blocks.

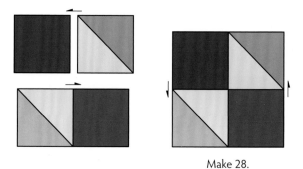

Make 28.

Making the Four-Patch Cornerstones

See "Collapsing Seam Allowances" at left for a helpful tip about pressing the completed block. Lay out four light 2½" squares in two rows. Sew the squares into rows. Join the rows to make a four-patch Cornerstone block. The block should measure 4½" square, including seam allowances. Make a total of four blocks.

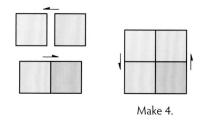

Make 4.

Assembling the Quilt Top

1 Lay out the Star blocks in six rows of six blocks each. Sew the blocks together into rows. Join the rows to complete the center of the quilt top, which should measure 48½" square, including seam allowances.

2 Sew 24-unit strips to the left and right sides of the quilt-top center, paying attention to the direction of the flying-geese units.

3 Join six Cotton Reel blocks, rotating every other block, to make a side border strip. Make two and sew them to the left and right sides of the quilt-top center. The quilt top should now measure 72½" × 48½", including seam allowances.

4 Join two four-unit flying-geese strips, two Cornerstone blocks, and one 24-unit flying-geese strip to make a border. Make two and sew them to the top and bottom of the quilt top, noting the direction of the flying-geese units.

5 Join eight Cotton Reel blocks and two four-unit flying-geese strips to make the top border. Repeat to make a bottom border. Sew the border strips to the top and bottom of the quilt top.

6 Machine baste around the quilt top about ⅛" from the outer edges to stabilize the seams.

Finishing the Quilt

For detailed instructions on any of the finishing steps, go to ShopMartingale.com/HowtoQuilt for free information.

1 Layer the backing, batting, and quilt top; baste.

2 Quilt by hand or machine. The quilt shown is quilted with a feathered design in the Star blocks and straight and curved lines in the flying-geese units.

3 Use the navy 2"-wide bias strips to make the binding; attach it to the quilt.

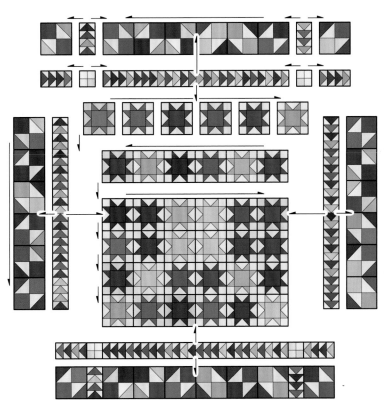

Quilt assembly

Petal Pushers

JILL FINLEY

Just try to resist this quilt with its big, mod flowers. Gently curved piecing makes the quilt unique, fun, and perfect for snuggling under. The curly vines lend movement and style to the overall design. Enjoy this fun little quilt!

Materials

Yardage is based on 42"-wide fabric.

2⅝ yards of white print for blocks and borders
2 yards of pink print for blocks and binding
1⅛ yards of green print for appliqués and outer border
3¼ yards of fabric for backing
59" × 59" piece of batting
⅜" bias-tape maker
Freezer paper
Jillily Studio Appli-Glue (optional)

Cutting

Use patterns A and B on pages 206 and 207 to make templates for cutting the piecing shapes, and use the circle pattern on page 207 for cutting the appliqué pieces. Transfer the alignment dots from the A and B templates to each fabric piece. All patchwork measurements include ¼"-wide seam allowances.

From the white print, cut:
5 strips, 6½" × 42"; trim 2 of the strips to 6½" × 36½"
16 of A
40 of B

From the pink print, cut:
20 of A
32 of B
6 strips, 2¼" × 42"

From the green print, cut:
1 strip, 18" × 42"; cut 10 *bias* strips, ⅞" × approximately 25"
6 strips, 2½" × 42"
5 of C

Making the Blocks

After sewing each seam, press seam allowances in the directions indicated by the arrows.

1 Place a white B piece on top of a pink A piece, right sides together. Match the center dot and pin in place. Now, match the outside dots of each piece, and pin. Gently ease the remainder of the curves together, matching the raw edges and pinning in place.

2 Stitch ¼" from the pinned edge along the seamline, pulling out each pin just before you reach it. As you stitch, watch the A fabric to be sure it doesn't shift. Guide and straighten both pieces of fabric as you stitch.

3 Repeat steps 1 and 2 to add a second white B piece to the opposite side of the pink A piece to make a pink petal unit. The unit should measure 6½" square, including seam allowances.

Finished quilt: 52½" × 52½"
Finished block: 12" × 12"

Pieced and appliquéd by Jill Finley;
quilted by Maika Christensen

4 Repeat steps 1–3 with the remaining pink A pieces and white B pieces to make a total of 20 pink petal units, and with the white A pieces and pink B pieces to make a total of 16 white petal units.

Make 20.   Make 16.

5 Lay out four pink petal units in two rows of two units each as shown. Sew the units in each row together. Sew the rows together. Repeat to make a total of five pink blocks. Repeat with the white petal units to make four white blocks.

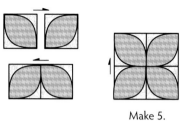

Make 5.

Make 4.

Assembling the Quilt Top

1 Refer to the quilt assembly diagram on page 205 to lay out the blocks in three rows of three blocks each, alternating the pink and white blocks in each row and from row to row. Sew the blocks in each row together. Press the seam allowances in opposite directions from row to row. Sew the rows together. Press the seam allowances in one direction. The quilt center should measure 36½" square, including seam allowances.

2 Sew the white 6½" × 36½" inner-border strips to the sides of the quilt center. Sew the remaining three white 6½" × 42" strips together end to end to make one long strip. From the pieced strip, cut two 48½"-long strips. Sew these strips to the top and bottom of the quilt center, which should now measure 48½" square, including seam allowances.

3 Sew the green 2½" × 42" outer-border strips together end to end to make one long strip. From the pieced strip, cut two 48½"-long strips and two 52½"-long strips. Sew the 48½"-long strips to the sides of the quilt top. Sew the 52½"-long strips to the top and bottom of the quilt top.

Appliquéing the Quilt

1 For more information on appliqué techniques, visit ShopMartingale.com/HowtoQuilt for free downloadable information. Prepare the appliqué C pieces. Baste a C piece to the center of each pink flower block using Jillily Studio Appli-Glue or the method of your choice.

2 Use the ⅞"-wide bias strips and the bias-tape maker to make 10 bias-tape pieces. Referring to the quilt photo on page 204, use the bias-tape pieces to create two vines on each pink flower. Shape the vines into curves and loops as shown in the photo, trimming as necessary. Carefully undo just enough of the seam where each vine meets the petals to stick the end of the vine into the seam. Hand stitch the opening closed. Turn the other end of the vine under, and glue baste in place.

3 Hand or machine stitch the appliqués in place.

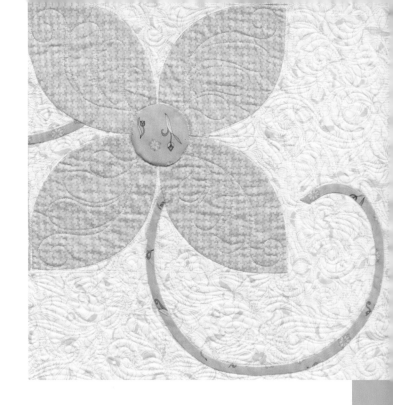

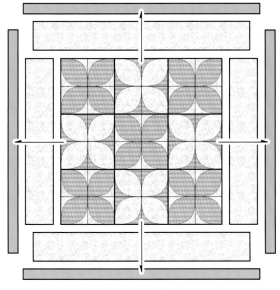

Quilt assembly

Finishing the Quilt

For detailed instructions on any of the finishing steps, go to ShopMartingale.com/HowtoQuilt for free information.

1 Layer the backing, batting, and quilt top; baste.

2 Quilt by hand or machine. The quilt shown is quilted with a feathered swirl motif in the petals and an allover swirl pattern in the background areas.

3 Use the pink 2¼"-wide strips to make the binding; attach it to the quilt.

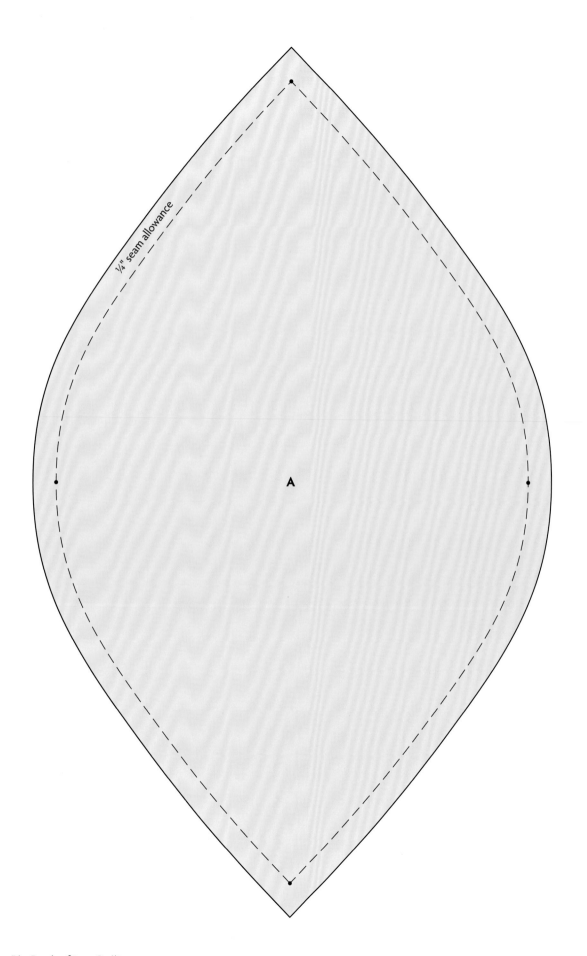

¼" seam allowance

A

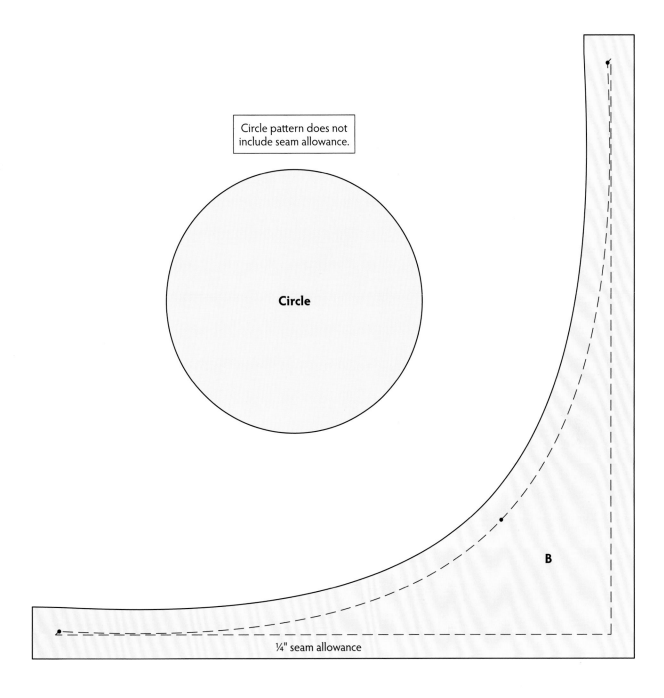

Circle pattern does not include seam allowance.

Circle

B

¼" seam allowance

Breaking Up

MELISSA CORRY

You can "break up" the chain of smaller solid squares with spunky prints and squares in alternate sizes. Dive into your scrap stash to make this adorable quilt.

Materials

Yardage is based on 42"-wide fabric.

⅝ yard of navy solid for blocks
3¼ yards of white solid for block backgrounds
1 yard *total* of assorted prints for blocks
⅝ yard of fabric for binding
3⅔ yards of fabric for backing
63" × 81" piece of batting

Cutting

All measurements include ¼"-wide seam allowances.

From the navy solid, cut:
6 strips, 2½" × 42"

From the white solid, cut:
2 strips, 16½" × 42"; crosscut into 31 rectangles, 2½" × 16½"
3 strips, 6½" × 42"
6 strips, 4½" × 42"; crosscut into 48 squares, 4½" × 4½"
9 strips, 2½" × 42"; crosscut 6 strips into 48 rectangles, 2½" × 4½"

From the assorted prints, cut:
48 squares, 4½" × 4½"
20 squares, 2½" × 2½"

From the binding fabric, cut:
7 strips, 2½" × 42"

Add Variety

Using precuts is a great way to add lots of variety in your quilt. Breaking Up is 5"-square or charm-pack friendly. So grab a stack or two of squares and start cutting.

Making the A Blocks

After sewing each seam, press seam allowances in the directions indicated by the arrows.

1 Sew a navy 2½" × 42" strip and a white 6½" × 42" strip together as shown. Make three strip sets. Cut 48 segments, 2½" wide.

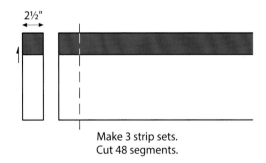

Make 3 strip sets.
Cut 48 segments.

2 Sew two white 2½" × 4½" rectangles and one print 4½" square together as shown. Make 24 units.

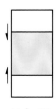

Make 24.

209

Making the B Blocks

1. Sew a navy 2½" × 42" strip and a white 2½" × 42" strip together lengthwise. Make three strip sets. Cut 48 segments, 2½" wide.

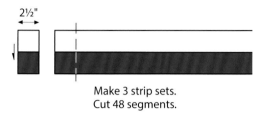

Make 3 strip sets.
Cut 48 segments.

2. Pin and sew two segments together, rotating them as shown to make a four-patch unit. Make 24 four-patch units.

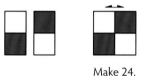

Make 24.

3. Pin and sew one four-patch unit, two white 4½" squares, and one print 4½" square together to make block B, which should measure 8½" square, including seam allowances. Make 24 blocks.

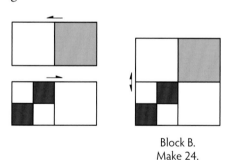

Block B.
Make 24.

Making the AB Blocks

Lay out two A blocks and two B blocks as shown. Sew the blocks together into rows. Pin and sew the rows together to make block AB, which should measure 16½" square, including seam allowances. Make 12 blocks.

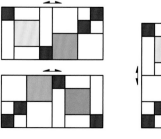

Block AB.
Make 12.

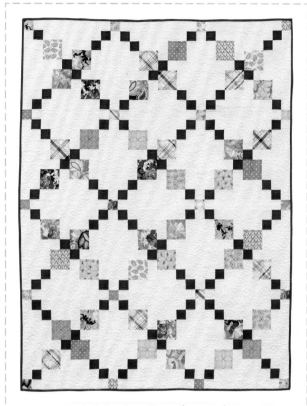

Finished quilt: 56½" × 74½"

Finished block: 16" × 16"

Fabrics are Vintage Verona by Emily Taylor Design for Riley Blake Designs

3. Pin and sew segments from step 1 to opposite sides of a unit from step 2 to complete block A, which should measure 8½" square, including seam allowances. Make 24 blocks.

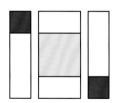

Block A.
Make 24.

Assembling the Quilt Top

1 Lay out the AB blocks in four rows with three blocks per row, rotating the blocks as shown in the assembly diagram below. Add the white 2½" × 16½" rectangles and the print 2½" squares around the blocks to create the sashing.

2 Sew the sashing rectangles and print squares into rows. Pin and sew the sashing rectangles and AB blocks into rows.

3 Pin and sew the rows together, finishing the quilt top.

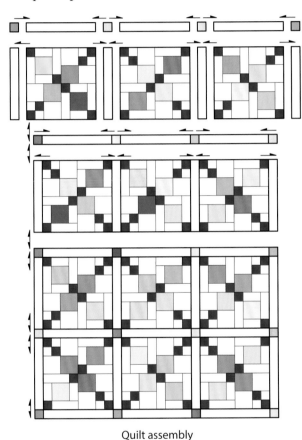

Quilt assembly

Finishing the Quilt

For detailed instructions on any of the finishing steps, go to ShopMartingale.com/HowtoQuilt for free information.

1 Layer the backing, batting, and quilt top; baste.

2 Quilt by hand or machine. The quilt shown is quilted with a traveling curl throughout the background and echo quilted arches in the print and navy.

3 Use the 2½"-wide strips to make the binding; attach it to the quilt.

Cherry Fizz

PAT SLOAN

Stitch a fabulous bowl of fresh cherries to create a summer day full of memories! Pair the cherry blocks with the simple Chain block, and your beautiful pile of fabric will turn into a fantastic design in no time at all.

Materials

Yardage is based on 42"-wide fabric.

⅓ yard *each* of 3 assorted raspberry-red prints for Chain blocks

1¼ yards of yellow print #1 for blocks

1⅛ yards of yellow print #2 for blocks

1¼ yards of green print for stem and leaf appliqués, inner border, and single-fold binding

¼ yard *each* of 2 assorted green prints for stem and leaf appliqués

12" × 12" square *each* of 4 assorted cherry-red prints for cherry appliqués

2¼ yards of large-scale red print for outer border

5 yards of fabric for backing

80" × 80" piece of batting

3 yards of 17"-wide paper-backed fusible web

Cutting

From *each* of 2 raspberry-red prints, cut:

3 strips, 2½" × 42"; crosscut into 36 squares, 2½" × 2½" (72 total)

From the remaining raspberry-red print, cut:

3 strips, 2½" × 42"; crosscut into 45 squares, 2½" × 2½"

From yellow print #1, cut:

2 strips, 10½" × 42"; crosscut into 6 squares, 10½" × 10½"

28 rectangles, 2½" × 6½"

28 squares, 2½" × 2½"

From yellow print #2, cut:

2 strips, 10½" × 42"; crosscut into 6 squares, 10½" × 10½"

24 rectangles, 2½" × 6½"

24 squares, 2½" × 2½"

From the green print for appliqués, inner border, and binding, cut:

14 strips, 1½" × 42"

From the *lengthwise* grain of the large-scale red print, cut:

2 strips, 10½" × 72½"

2 strips, 10½" × 52½"

Making the Chain Blocks

After sewing each seam, press seam allowances in the directions indicated by the arrows.

1 Randomly select nine assorted raspberry-red 2½" squares, four assorted yellow 2½" squares, and four assorted yellow 2½" × 6½" rectangles.

2 Arrange five raspberry-red squares and four yellow squares into three horizontal rows, alternating the colors in each row and from row to row. Sew the squares in each row together. Sew the rows together to make a nine-patch unit.

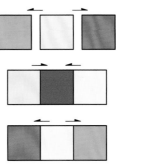 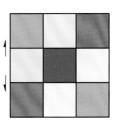

Finished quilt: 72½" × 72½"

Finished block: 10" × 10"

Quilted by Cindy and Dennis Dickinson

Making the Appliquéd Blocks

1 Use your favorite appliqué method and the patterns on page 216 to prepare the appliqués from the fabrics indicated on the patterns. Remove the paper backing from each shape.

2 Position the prepared appliqué shapes on a yellow 10½" square in the following order. Center a cluster of three leaves on the upper third of the square. Place three stems and three cherries, tucking the stem ends under the leaves and cherries. Fuse the appliqués in place. Repeat to make a total of 12 appliquéd blocks.

Appliqué placement

3 Blanket-stitch around the outer edges of each shape on each block.

Assembling the Quilt Top

1 Arrange the Chain blocks and appliquéd blocks in five rows of five blocks each, alternating the blocks and yellow background fabric in each row and from row to row. Sew the blocks in each row together. Join the rows. The quilt top should measure 50½" square, including seam allowances.

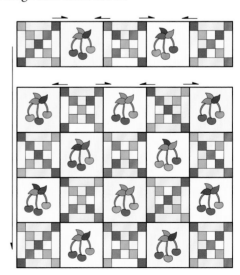

3 Join yellow rectangles to the sides of the nine-patch unit. Add a raspberry-red square to each end of the remaining yellow rectangles. Join these pieced strips to the top and bottom edges of the nine-patch unit to complete the block, which should measure 10½" square, including seam allowances.

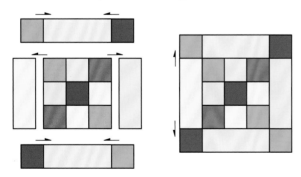

4 Repeat steps 1–3 to make a total of 13 Chain blocks.

2 Join six of the green 1½" × 42" strips end to end to make one long strip. From the pieced strip, cut two inner-border strips, 1½" × 50½". Refer to the assembly diagram below to sew the strips to the sides of the quilt top. From the remainder of the pieced strip, cut two inner-border strips, 1½" × 52½". Join these strips to the top and bottom edges of the quilt top.

3 Sew the red 10½" × 52½" outer-border strips to the sides of the quilt top. Join the red 10½" × 72½" outer-border strips to the top and bottom edges of the quilt top.

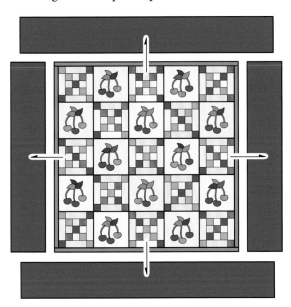

Quilt assembly

Finishing the Quilt

For detailed instructions on any of the finishing steps, go to ShopMartingale.com/HowtoQuilt for free information.

1 Layer the backing, batting, and quilt top; baste.

2 Quilt by hand or machine. This quilt is outline quilted around the appliqués and a meandering design is quilted in the background.

3 Use the remaining green 1½"-wide strips to make the binding; attach it to the quilt.

Little Packages

You know that saying, "Good things come in little packages"? Well, if this 72" square quilt is too big for your needs, consider making a smaller version. If you use five Chain blocks and four Cherry blocks, you can have a 30" square quilt in no time! Add a border if you want it a little bigger, or just quilt and bind for an adorable little wall hanging.

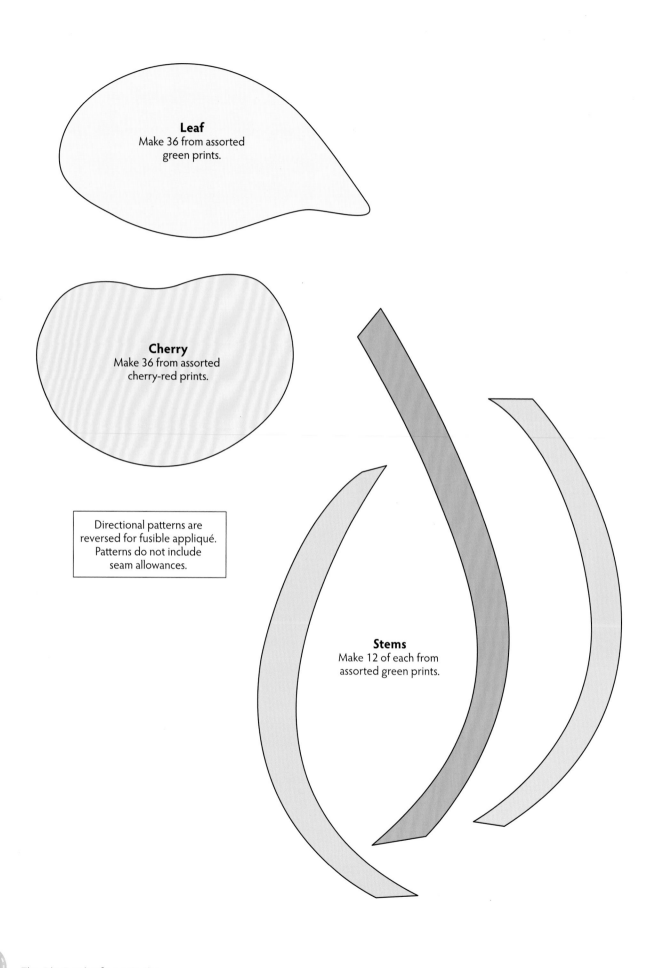

Leaf
Make 36 from assorted
green prints.

Cherry
Make 36 from assorted
cherry-red prints.

Directional patterns are
reversed for fusible appliqué.
Patterns do not include
seam allowances.

Stems
Make 12 of each from
assorted green prints.

Dominoes

PAT WYS

The classic granny square gets a fun, up-to-date touch when we play dominoes with fabric. This quilt shimmers and seems to pulsate as the dark, medium, and light values change across the surface.

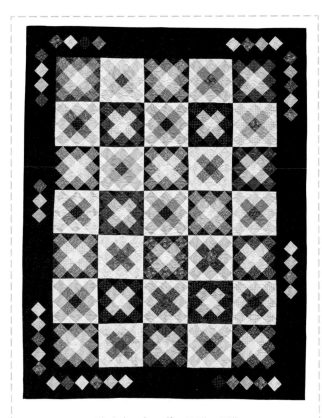

Finished quilt: 54" × 71"
Finished block: 8½" × 8½"

Pieced by Karin Efman; quilted by Leisa Wiggley

Materials

Yardage is based on 42"-wide fabric.

3 yards of black tone on tone for blocks, borders, and binding

1¼ yards *total* of assorted light neutral prints for blocks and pieced border

1¼ yards *total* of assorted medium neutral prints for blocks and pieced border

1 yard *total* of assorted white tone on tones for blocks and pieced border

¼ yard *total* of assorted dark neutral prints for blocks and pieced border

3½ yards of fabric for backing

60" × 77" piece of batting

12" or 14" square ruler

How to Begin

"Time spent planning will reward you in the construction process," says quilt designer Pat Wys. "Before you start sewing, brew yourself a cup of tea or coffee, sit down, and read the pattern. Make notes and plan ahead. An organized project is a project less likely to have problems. Ask me how I know!"

Cutting

All measurements include ¼"-wide seam allowances. Keep the half-square and quarter-square triangles together for the block corners and sides.

From the assorted white tone on tones, cut:

18 squares, 2½" × 2½"

17 *matching sets* of:

    2 squares, 2½" × 2½" (34 total); cut the squares in half diagonally to yield 4 triangles (68 total)

    2 squares, 4¼" × 4¼" (34 total); cut into quarters diagonally to yield 8 triangles (136 total)

10 squares, 2¼" × 2¼"

From the assorted light prints, cut:

18 sets of 4 *matching* squares, 2½" × 2½" (72 total)

17 sets of 8 *matching* squares, 2½" × 2½" (136 total)

10 squares, 2¼" × 2¼"

From the assorted medium prints, cut:

18 sets of 8 *matching* squares, 2½" × 2½" (144 total)

17 sets of 4 *matching* squares, 2½" × 2½" (68 total)

10 squares, 2¼" × 2¼"

From the black tone on tone, cut:

3 strips, 2½" × 42"; crosscut into 36 squares, 2½" × 2½". Cut the squares in half diagonally to yield 72 triangles.

4 strips, 4¼" × 42"; crosscut into 36 squares, 4¼" × 4¼". Cut the squares into quarters diagonally to yield 144 triangles.

12 strips, 2" × 42"

4 strips, 3" × 42"; crosscut into:

    1 strip, 3" × 26"

    1 strip, 3" × 25½"

    1 strip, 3" × 18½"

    1 strip, 3" × 18"

    2 strips, 3" × 15½"

    4 squares, 3" × 3"

3 strips, 3¾" × 42"; crosscut into 25 squares, 3¾" × 3¾". Cut the squares into quarters diagonally to yield 100 triangles (2 are extra).

266" of 2½"-wide bias binding

From the assorted dark prints, cut:

17 squares, 2½" × 2½"

10 squares, 2¼" × 2¼"

Making the Blocks

You'll need 18 blocks with a white center and 17 blocks with a dark center. Each block is made up of four fabrics: a white print, light print, medium print, and dark print. After sewing each seam, press seam allowances as indicated by the arrows.

1 To make the dark-background block, choose one white 2½" square, four matching light 2½" squares, eight matching medium 2½" squares, eight black 4¼" triangles, and four black 2½" triangles. Arrange the squares and triangles in diagonal rows as shown.

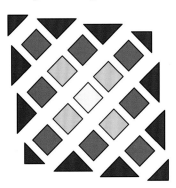

2 Sew squares and triangles in rows; join the rows. The triangles are slightly oversized; you'll trim the blocks later. Make 18 dark-background blocks.

Make 18.

3 To make a light-background block, choose one dark 2½" square, four matching medium 2½" squares, eight matching light 2½" squares, and a matching set of eight white 4¼" triangles and four 2½" triangles. Arrange the squares and triangles in diagonal rows; sew the blocks together as before. Make a total of 17 light-background blocks.

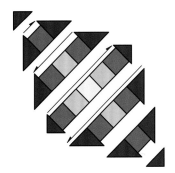

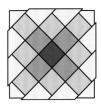

Make 17.

4 Press the blocks carefully and square them up by trimming them with your square ruler and rotary cutter. Lay a square ruler over the block. Make sure you leave ¼" seam allowance beyond the points of the squares. Square the blocks to 9" × 9".

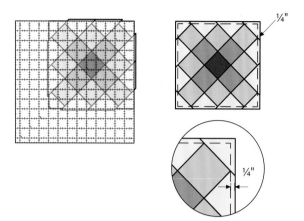

Assembling the Quilt Top

1 Arrange the blocks in seven horizontal rows of five blocks each. Rows 1, 3, 5, and 7 begin and end with a dark-background block. Rows 2, 4, and 6 begin and end with a light-background block. The quilt should now be 43" × 60", including seam allowances.

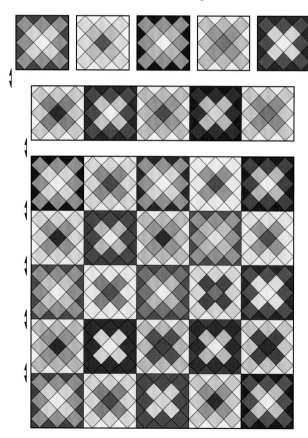

Quilt assembly

2 Sew the 12 black 2" × 42" strips together with diagonal seams to make one long strip. Then measure the length of the quilt top through the center; trim and add the side borders. Measure the width of the quilt including the borders just added; trim and add the top and bottom borders.

3 Piece the middle border using 2¼" squares of assorted values and the black 3¾" triangles. Sew triangles to the left and right sides of three squares as shown. Join these units and two additional 3¾" triangles to make a pieced strip. Square the ends of the strip by cutting ¼" beyond the point of the square, preserving the ¼" seam allowance.

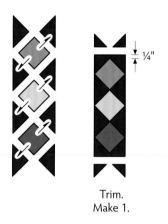

Trim.
Make 1.

4 Repeat step 3 to make four strips with four squares, three strips with five squares, and one strip with six squares.

Make 4.　　Make 3.　　Make 1.

Differences!

If the center of your quilt did not measure exactly 43" × 60", you may need to make a few adjustments in the lengths of the black tone-on-tone border strips. Be sure to measure through the center of your quilt for each border. You may have to add or subtract from the spacer strips between the pieced units. Simply add up the lengths of your pieced units and spacer strips. They should equal the length and width of your quilt top. It's not difficult and there will be no visual difference between your quilt and this one.

5 After you complete the strips of on-point squares, sew border strips for the quilt referring to the diagram, adding the black 3"-wide strips and 3" squares as specified. Sew the left and right side borders to the quilt first, then add the top and bottom borders. Press.

6 Measure, cut, and sew the black 2"-wide outer border to each side of the quilt.

Finishing the Quilt

For detailed instructions on any of the finishing steps, go to ShopMartingale.com/HowtoQuilt for free information.

1 Layer the backing, batting, and quilt top; baste.

2 Quilt by hand or machine. The quilt shown is quilted with an overall paisley pattern.

3 Use the black 2½"-wide bias strips to make the binding; attach it to the quilt.

Adding borders

Raise the Roof

CARRIE NELSON

Add sparkle to the classic Barn Raising setting, in which dark and light halves of Log Cabin blocks alternate to form radiating rows from the quilt center, by inserting stars.

Materials

Yardage is based on 42"-wide fabric. Fat quarters are 18" × 21".

14 fat quarters of assorted light prints for blocks and inner border

19 fat quarters of assorted medium and dark prints (collectively referred to as *dark*) for blocks and outer border

¾ yard of brown print for binding

4¾ yards of fabric for backing

81" × 81" piece of batting

Cutting

All measurements include ¼"-wide seam allowances.

From *each* of 9 assorted light fat quarters, cut:

1 strip, 5¼" × 21"; crosscut into:
    2 squares, 5¼" × 5¼" (18 total; 2 are extra)
    3 squares, 2⅞" × 2⅞" (27 total)
    1 strip, 1½" × 10" (9 total; 1 is extra)
1 strip, 2⅞" × 21"; crosscut into:
    5 squares, 2⅞" × 2⅞" (45 total)
    2 squares, 2½" × 2½" (18 total; 2 are extra)
6 strips, 1½" × 21" (54 total)

From *each* of 4 assorted light fat quarters, cut:

1 strip, 5¼" × 21"; crosscut into 3 squares, 5¼" × 5¼" (12 total)
2 strips, 2⅞" × 21"; crosscut into:
    10 squares, 2⅞" × 2⅞" (40 total)
    4 squares, 2½" × 2½" (16 total)
2 strips, 1½" × 21" (8 total)

From *1* assorted light fat quarter, cut:

2 strips, 5¼" × 21"; crosscut into 4 squares, 5¼" × 5¼"

From *each* of 16 assorted dark fat quarters, cut:

1 strip, 5¼" × 21"; crosscut into:
    2 squares, 5¼" × 5¼" (32 total)
    1 strip, 2⅞" × 10"; crosscut into 3 squares, 2⅞" × 2⅞" (48 total)
    1 strip, 1½" × 10" (16 total)
1 strip, 2⅞" × 21"; crosscut into:
    4 squares, 2⅞" × 2⅞" (64 total)
    2 squares, 2½" × 2½" (32 total)
    2 rectangles, 1½" × 2½" (32 total)
6 strips, 1½" × 21" (96 total; 1 is extra)

From *each* of 3 assorted dark fat quarters, cut:

9 strips, 1½" × 21" (27 total)

From the brown print, cut:

315" of 2"-wide bias binding

ADDITIONAL CUTTING FOR LOG CABIN BLOCKS

Set aside 14 light 1½" × 21" strips for the inner border and 66 dark 1½" × 21" strips for the outer border.

From the 8 light 1½" × 10" strips, cut:

32 rectangles, 1½" × 2½"

From 16 light 1½" × 21" strips, cut each strip into:

2 rectangles, 1½" × 3½" (32 total)
2 rectangles, 1½" × 4½" (32 total)

From 32 light 1½" × 21" strips, cut each strip into:

1 rectangle, 1½" × 5½" (32 total)
1 rectangle, 1½" × 6½" (32 total)
1 rectangle, 1½" × 7½" (32 total)

From the 16 dark 1½" × 10" strips, cut:

16 rectangles, 1½" × 8½"

Continued on page 224

Finished quilt: 74½" × 74½"

Finished blocks: 8" × 8"

Quilted by Diane Tricka

Continued from page 223

From 32 dark 1½" × 21" strips, cut *each* strip into:
1 rectangle, 1½" × 3½" (32 total)
1 rectangle, 1½" × 4½" (32 total)
1 rectangle, 1½" × 5½" (32 total)
1 rectangle, 1½" × 6½" (32 total)

From 16 dark 1½" × 21" strips, cut *each* strip into:
1 rectangle, 1½" × 7½" (16 total)
1 rectangle, 1½" × 8½" (16 total)

From 8 dark 1½" × 21" strips, cut *each* strip into:
2 rectangles, 1½" × 7½" (16 total)

Making the Star Blocks

Use a scant ¼" seam allowance throughout the project. After sewing each seam, press seam allowances in the directions indicated by the arrows.

FLYING-GEESE UNITS

1 On the wrong side of each light 2⅞" square, draw a diagonal line from corner to corner using a permanent pen, pencil, or chalk marker. Set aside 48 squares for making half-square-triangle units.

2 With right sides together, place two marked squares on opposite corners of a dark 5¼" square as shown. The points of the small squares will overlap and the drawn line should extend across the large square from corner to corner.

3 Stitch a scant ¼" from both sides of the drawn line. Cut the squares apart on the drawn line.

4 With right sides together, place a remaining marked square on the corner of each piece. The drawn line should extend from the point of the corner to the point between the two small triangles. Stitch a scant ¼" from both sides of the drawn line. Cut the unit apart on the drawn line. The flying-geese units should measure 2½" × 4½". Make 16 sets of four matching units (64 total).

Make 64.

224 The Big Book of Lap Quilts

5 On the wrong side of 64 dark 2⅞" squares, draw a diagonal line from corner to corner using a permanent pen, pencil, or chalk marker. Repeat steps 2–4 using the marked squares and the light 5¼" squares to make 16 sets of four matching units (64 total).

Make 64.

HALF-SQUARE-TRIANGLE UNITS

Using the marked squares from step 1 of "Flying-Geese Units," layer a marked square and a dark 2⅞" square, right sides together, and align the raw edges. Stitch a scant ¼" from both sides of the drawn line. Cut the squares apart on the drawn line to make two half-square-triangle units. The units should measure 2½" square. Make a total of 96 units. Set aside 32 of them for the Log Cabin blocks.

2½"

2½"

Make 96.

QUARTER-SQUARE-TRIANGLE UNITS

1 On the wrong side of eight light 5¼" and eight dark 5¼" squares, draw a diagonal line from corner to corner using a permanent pen, pencil, or chalk marker.

2 Layer a marked light square and a second light 5¼" square, right sides together, and align the raw edges. Stitch a scant ¼" from both sides of the drawn line. Cut the squares apart on the drawn line to make two half-square-triangle units. Make 16 light units.

Make 16.

3 Repeat step 2, using a marked dark square and a second dark 5¼" square to make a dark half-square-triangle unit. Make 16 units.

Make 16.

4 On the wrong side of each light half-square-triangle unit, draw a diagonal line from corner to corner across the seam as shown. Place a light and a dark half-square-triangle unit right sides together, with the light unit on top, and align the raw edges.

5 Butt the diagonal seams against each other and stitch a scant ¼" from both sides of the drawn line. Cut the squares apart on the drawn line. Each pair of squares will make two matching quarter-square-triangle units, which should measure 4½" square. Make a total of 32 units.

Make 32.

ASSEMBLING THE STAR BLOCKS

For each block, you'll need the following pieces:

- **Light:** one 2½" square
- **Dark:** one 2½" square
- **Flying-geese units:** two different light 2½" × 4½" units and two different dark 2½" × 4½" units
- **Half-square-triangle units:** two different 2½" × 2½" units
- **Quarter-square-triangle units:** one 4½" × 4½" unit

Lay out the pieces in three rows as shown to make a half light/half dark Star block. Sew the pieces together into rows. Join the rows. The block should measure 8½" square, including seam allowances. Make 32 Star blocks.

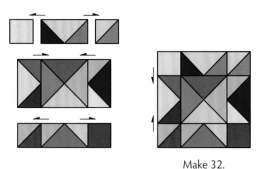

Make 32.

Making the Log Cabin Blocks

1 Join a light 1½" × 2½" rectangle to the light side of each 2½" half-square-triangle unit as shown. Sew a light 1½" × 3½" rectangle to the bottom of the unit. Make 32.

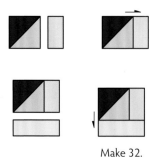

Make 32.

2 Join a dark 1½" × 3½" rectangle to the left side of the center unit as shown. Sew a dark 1½" × 4½" rectangle to the top of the center unit. Make 32.

Make 32.

3 Continue sewing rectangles to each unit in the following order:

- **Light:** 1½" × 4½" rectangle
- **Light:** 1½" × 5½" rectangle
- **Dark:** 1½" × 5½" rectangle
- **Dark:** 1½" × 6½" rectangle

- **Light:** 1½" × 6½" rectangle
- **Light:** 1½" × 7½" rectangle
- **Dark:** 1½" × 7½" rectangle
- **Dark:** 1½" × 8½" rectangle

Each block should measure 8½" square, including seam allowances. Make a total of 32 Log Cabin blocks.

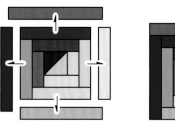

Make 32.

MAKING THE OUTER BORDER

1 Randomly divide the remaining dark 1½" × 21" strips into six groups of 11 strips each. Join one group of strips along their long edges to make a strip set that is 11½" × 21". Make six strip sets. From the strip sets, cut 24 segments, 4½" × 11½".

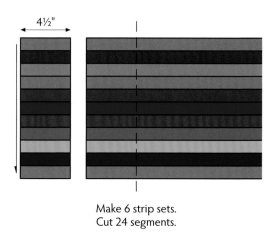

Make 6 strip sets.
Cut 24 segments.

2 Separate the segments into four groups, each consisting of six different segments. Join the segments from one group to make a 66½"-long strip. Make a total of four strips.

Make 4.

3 Sort the dark 1½" × 2½" rectangles into four groups of eight rectangles each. Lay out one group of rectangles as shown. Sew the rectangles into

pairs to make four units, 2½" square. Join the units as shown to make a corner block. The block should measure 4½" square, including seam allowances. Make four blocks.

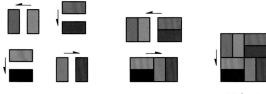

Make 4.

Assembling the Quilt Top

Pay attention to the placement of the light and dark halves of the blocks.

1 Lay out the Star and Log Cabin blocks in eight rows of eight blocks each, alternating them as shown in the quilt assembly diagram below. Sew the blocks together into rows, and then join the rows.

2 For the inner border, join the remaining light 1½" × 21" strips end to end. Measure the length of the quilt top through the center; it should measure 64½", including seam allowances. From the long strip, cut two strips to this measurement and sew them to opposite sides of the quilt top.

3 Measure the width of the quilt top through the center; it should measure 66½" including the side borders and seam allowances. From the remainder of the light strip, cut two strips to this measurement and sew them to the top and bottom of the quilt top to complete the inner border.

4 Sew outer-border strips to opposite sides of the quilt top. Join corner blocks to the ends of the two remaining outer-border strips. Sew these strips to the top and bottom of the quilt top.

5 Machine baste around the quilt top about ⅛" from the outer edges to stabilize the seams.

Finishing the Quilt

For detailed instructions on any of the finishing steps, go to ShopMartingale.com/HowtoQuilt for free information.

1 Layer the backing, batting, and quilt top; baste.

2 Quilt by hand or machine. The quilt shown is quilted with feathers, curves, and radiating straight lines.

3 Use the brown 2"-wide bias strips to make the binding; attach it to the quilt.

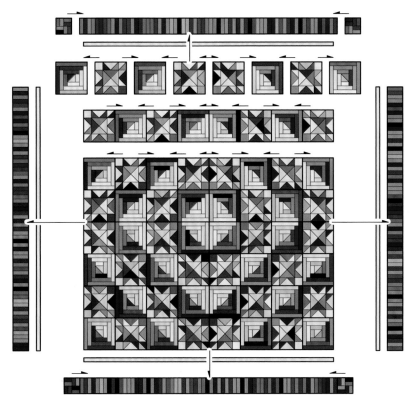

Quilt assembly

The Comfort Quilt

AMY ELLIS

There's something special about a scrappy cross quilt. This design was inspired by the history of the Red Cross and the quilts that were auctioned off as wartime fund-raisers. A simple Cross block was surrounded by donors' signatures, filling the background fabrics with ink or red floss–embroidered names. Comfort and love were stitched into each block. Make this project with a special someone in mind or to have ready for a friend in need.

Materials

Yardage is based on 42"-wide fabric.

3½ yards *total* of assorted light prints for blocks
1⅛ yards *total* of assorted medium to dark prints for blocks (collectively referred to as *dark*)
⅞ yard of light print #1 for wide horizontal panel
½ yard *each* of light prints #2 and #3 for narrow horizontal panels
⅝ yard of fabric for binding
4⅝ yards of fabric for backing
67" × 82" piece of batting

Cutting

All measurements include ¼"-wide seam allowances. Keep matching sets of rectangles together as you cut. See "One at a Time" at right for more information.

From the assorted light prints, cut:
228 squares, 3" × 3"
396 squares, 1¾" × 1¾"
228 squares, 1½" × 1½"
396 squares, 1" × 1"

From the assorted dark prints, cut:
57 matching sets of 2 rectangles, 1½" × 2", and 1 rectangle, 1½" × 4½"
99 matching sets of 2 rectangles, 1" × 1¼", and 1 rectangle, 1" × 2½"

From light print #1, cut:
2 strips, 12½" × 42"

From *each* of light prints #2 and #3, cut:
2 strips, 6½" × 42"

From the binding fabric, cut:
7 strips, 2¼" × 42"

One at a Time

For each large Cross block, you'll need the following:

- 2 matching dark 1½" × 2" rectangles and 1 matching 1½" × 4½" rectangle
- 4 assorted light 1½" squares
- 4 assorted light 3" squares

For each small Cross block, you'll need the following:

- 2 matching dark 1" × 1¼" rectangles and 1 matching 1" × 2½" rectangle
- 4 assorted light 1" squares
- 4 assorted light 1¾" squares

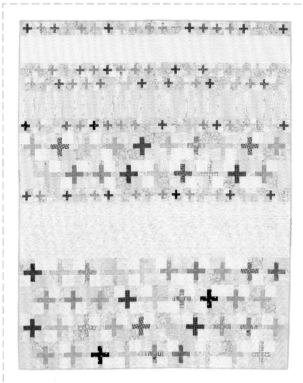

Finished quilt: 60½" × 75½"

Large Cross block: 6" × 6"

Small Cross block: 3" × 3"

Making the Large Cross Blocks

After sewing each seam, press seam allowances in the directions indicated by the arrows.

1 Sew a light 1½" square to each end of a dark 1½" × 4½" rectangle.

2 Sew a light 1½" square to one end of a dark 1½" × 2" rectangle. Make two units.

Make 2.

3 Sew a light 3" square to each side of the units from step 2.

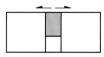

4 Sew the units made in step 3 to opposite sides of the rectangle unit from step 1 to complete the block, which should measure 6½" square, including seam allowances.

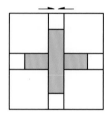

5 Repeat steps 1–4 to make a total of 57 large Cross blocks.

Making the Small Cross Blocks

1 Sew a light 1" square to each end of a dark 1" × 2½" rectangle.

2 Sew a light 1" square to one end of a dark 1" × 1¼" rectangle. Make two units.

Make 2.

3 Sew a light 1¾" square to each side of the units from step 2.

4 Sew the units made in step 3 to opposite sides of the rectangle unit from step 1 to complete the block, which should measure 3½" square, including seam allowances.

5 Repeat steps 1–4 to make a total of 99 small Cross blocks.

Assembling the Quilt Top

1 Lay out four rows of 20 small blocks each, one row of 19 small blocks, three rows of 10 large blocks each, and three rows of 9 large blocks each, referring to the quilt assembly diagram. Rotate the blocks as needed so the seam allowances nest together. Pin and sew the blocks together in rows, pressing the seam allowances in alternate directions from row to row.

2 Measure the width of the 20-block rows and 10-block rows. They should measure 60½", including seam allowances. If they don't, just make sure that all the rows are the same length and use that measurement in the next steps.

3 Sew two matching light 6½" × 42" strips together using a diagonal seam, and cut to measure 60½" or the width of your quilt rows. Make two. From the excess fabric, cut six rectangles, 3½" × 6½", and two rectangles, 2" × 3½"; these will fill in the ends of the shorter block rows as you assemble the quilt top.

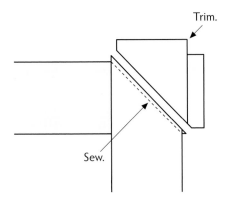

4 Sew the two light 12½" × 42" strips together using a diagonal seam, and cut to 60½" or the width of your quilt.

5 Sew the rectangles cut in step 3 to each end of the shorter block rows.

6 Pin and sew the rows together to complete the quilt top.

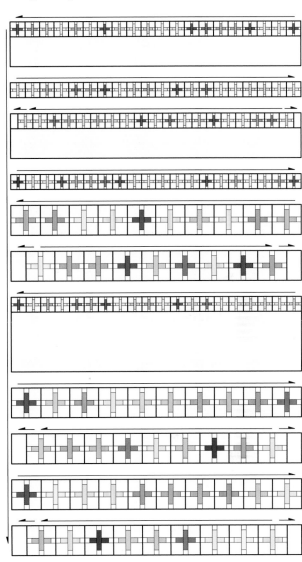

Quilt assembly

Finishing the Quilt

For detailed instructions on any of the finishing steps, go to ShopMartingale.com/HowtoQuilt for free information.

1 Layer the backing, batting, and quilt top; baste.

2 Quilt by hand or machine. The quilt shown is quilted with zigzags and a diamond pattern.

3 Use the 2¼"-wide strips to make the binding; attach it to the quilt.

Fresh Air

PAT SLOAN

Have you looked at a quilt made with equilateral or 60° triangles and thought, "Oh my, that looks too hard!"? This is one shape where a purpose-made ruler is a lifesaver. The easiest way to start is by arranging the triangles in rows. And why not spice things up with random color placement? If you like a more orderly look, just alternate the white triangles with the printed triangles and make this design your own.

Materials

Yardage is based on 42"-wide fabric.

¼ yard *each* of 15 assorted prints for triangles
2⅛ yards of gray floral for triangles and outer border
1⅛ yards of white-on-white print for triangles
⅞ yard of peach print for inner border and binding
3¾ yards of fabric for backing
68" × 78" piece of batting
Template plastic*
60° ruler (optional)*

Template plastic is not required if using a 60° ruler. The ruler needs to have a vertical centerline and measurements along the horizontal lines, not side measurements.

Cutting

All measurements include ¼"-wide seam allowances.

From *each* assorted print, cut:
1 strip, 5½" × 42" (15 total)

From the *lengthwise* grain of the gray floral, cut:
2 strips, 8½" × 68½"
2 strips, 8½" × 42¾"
1 strip, 5½" × 42"

From the white-on-white print, cut:
6 strips, 5½" × 42"

From the peach print, cut:
5 strips, 1½" × 42"
7 strips, 2¼" × 42"

Assembling the Quilt Top

Refer to the photo on page 234 for color placement guidance throughout. After sewing each seam, press seam allowances in the directions indicated by the arrows.

1 Use the triangle pattern on page 235 to make a template. Use the template (or a 60° ruler) to cut 97 triangles from the print and floral 5½"-wide strips. In the same way, cut 53 triangles from the white strips. If using a 60° ruler, align the 5½" line with the edge of the strip.

2 Randomly lay out the print and white triangles in 10 rows as shown in the row assembly diagram on page 234. Each row contains 15 triangles. Sew the triangles together in rows.

Finished quilt: 58¾" × 68½"

4 Trim the sides of the quilt top, making sure to leave ¼" of fabric beyond the last seam intersection for seam allowance. The quilt top should measure 40¾" × 50½", including seam allowances.

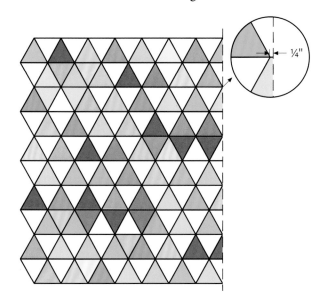

3 Sew the rows together. Press.

Row assembly

5 Sew the peach 1½"-wide strips together end to end. From the pieced strip, cut two 40¾"-long strips; sew them to the top and bottom of the quilt top. From the remaining pieced strip, cut two 52½"-long strips; sew them to the sides. The quilt should measure 42¾" × 52½", including seam allowances.

6 Sew the floral 42¾"-long strips to the top and bottom of the quilt top. Sew the floral 68½"-long strips to the sides of the quilt top.

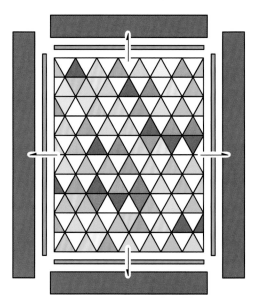

Quilt assembly

Finishing the Quilt

For detailed instructions on any of the finishing steps, go to ShopMartingale.com/HowtoQuilt for free information.

1 Layer the backing, batting, and quilt top; baste.

2 Quilt by hand or machine. This quilt is quilted with a Baptist fan design.

3 Use the peach 2¼"-wide strips to make the binding; attach it to the quilt.

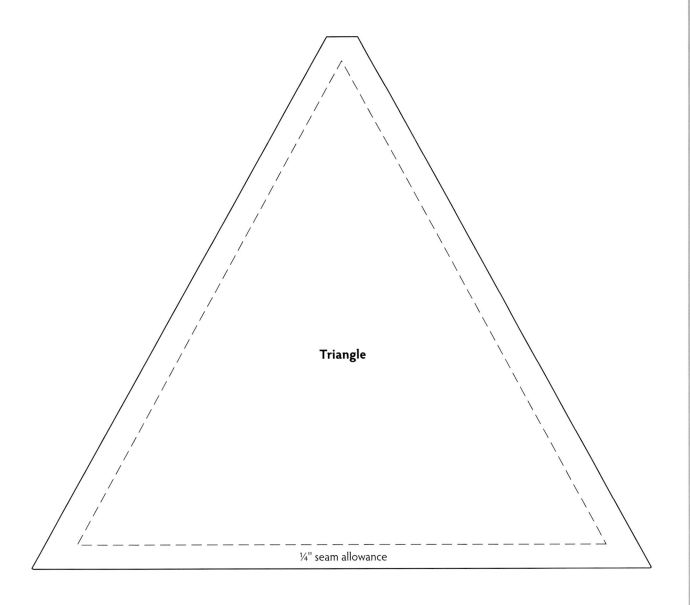

Triangle

¼" seam allowance

The Simplest Sampler

PETA PEACE

When made from a collection of prints, the Simplest Sampler has the look of a sampler but there's one big difference: it's made with just one block, so it's a dream to piece and finish.

Materials

Yardage is based on 42"-wide fabric.

1¾ yards of white solid for blocks

36 precut squares, 10" × 10", of assorted prints for blocks

2⅛ yards of aqua solid for background, sashing, and border

⅝ yard of teal diagonal stripe for binding

3¾ yards of fabric for backing

67" × 74" piece of batting

Cutting

All measurements include ¼"-wide seam allowances.

From the white solid, cut:

6 strips, 3¼" × 42"; crosscut into 72 squares, 3¼" × 3¼"

3 strips, 2½" × 42"; crosscut into 36 squares, 2½" × 2½"

3 strips, 10" × 42"; crosscut into 72 strips, 1½" × 10"

From *each* of the 36 precut squares, cut:

4 squares, 3¼" × 3¼" (144 total)

1 square, 2½" × 2½" (36 total)

2 strips, 1½" × 10" (72 total)

2 squares, 1½" × 1½" (72 total; 16 are extra)

From the aqua solid, cut:

6 strips, 3¼" × 42"; crosscut into 72 squares, 3¼" × 3¼"

5 strips, 6½" × 42"; crosscut into 127 strips, 1½" × 6½"

7 strips, 2½" × 42"

From the teal diagonal stripe, cut:

7 strips, 2½" × 42"

Making Block A

Use a single print within each block; each print will be used in two blocks (one A block and one B block). After sewing each seam, press seam allowances in the directions indicated by the arrows.

1 Draw a diagonal line from corner to corner on the wrong side of two 3¼" white squares.

2 Place a marked square on a 3¼" print square with right sides together. Pin the white square in place and sew a scant ¼" from the drawn line on both sides. Cut on the drawn line to yield two half-square-triangle units. Make four. Trim to 2½" square.

Make 4.

3 Sew a 1½" × 10" white strip to a 1½" × 10" print strip with right sides together. Crosscut the strip set into four segments, 2½" wide.

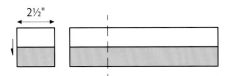

2½"

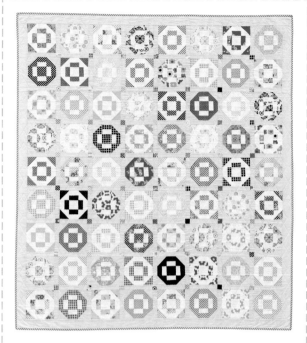

Finished quilt: 59½" × 66½"

Finished block: 6" × 6"

Pieced by Peta Peace;
quilted by Diane Farrugia

Making Block B

Block B is assembled in the same way as block A, with some fabric changes.

1 Repeat step 1 of "Making Block A," using 3¼" aqua squares in place of white squares. Draw a diagonal line from corner to corner on the wrong side of two 3¼" aqua squares.

2 When you assemble the block, use a print square at the center and change the positions of the half-square-triangle units and strip-set segments as shown to make a block measuring 6½" square, including seam allowances. Make 36 B blocks.

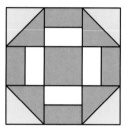

Make 36,
6½" × 6½".

Super Stripes

The binding for this quilt was cut from a print featuring diagonal stripes. If you want the same look from a fabric that has straight-grain stripes, cut the binding strips on the bias. You'll need to purchase more fabric, about ⅔ yard, and cut bias strips totaling about 265".

Assembling the Quilt Top

1 Referring to the quilt assembly diagram on page 239, arrange the A and B blocks in nine rows of eight blocks, alternating the A and B blocks. Place aqua 1½" × 6½" strips between blocks in each row. Sew the rows together to measure 6½" × 55½", including seam allowances.

4 Arrange the four half-square-triangle units, the four strip-set segments, and one 2½" white square as shown. Sew the units together in rows and then join the rows to make a block measuring 6½" square, including seam allowances. Make 36 A blocks.

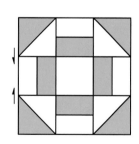
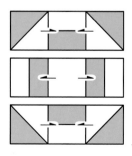

Make 36,
6½" × 6½".

2 Sew together eight aqua 1½" × 6½" strips and seven 1½" print squares as shown to make a sashing row. Make eight sashing rows measuring 1½" × 55½", including seam allowances.

3 Sew the rows together. Match the seams and pin at the intersections before sewing. The quilt center should measure 55½" × 62½", including seam allowances.

Adding the Border

1 Sew the seven aqua 2½" × 42" strips together end to end to make one long strip.

2 Cut two strips, 2½" × 62½", and sew them to opposite sides of the quilt center.

3 Cut two strips, 2½" × 59½", and sew them to the top and bottom edges of the quilt. The quilt top should measure 59½" × 66½".

Finishing the Quilt

For detailed instructions on any of the finishing steps, go to ShopMartingale.com/HowtoQuilt for free information.

1 Layer the backing, batting, and quilt top; baste.

2 Quilt by hand or machine. The quilt shown is quilted with a diamond pattern.

3 Use the teal 2½"-wide strips to make the binding; attach it to the quilt.

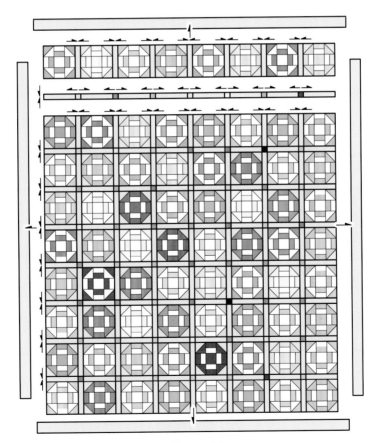

Quilt assembly

A world of creativity awaits inside these Martingale titles.

Find these books at your local quilt shop or at ShopMartingale.com.

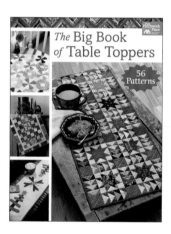

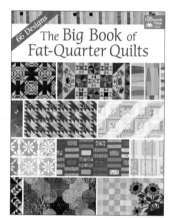

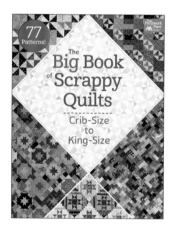

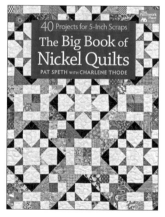